PATTON'S
TANK DRIVE
D-DAY TO VICTORY

Michael Green

MBI Publishing Company

Dedication

To my good friend James "Jimmy" H. Leach, DSC, Colonel, US Army (Retired),
for all his help and support during the completion of this book.

First published in 1995 by MBI Publishing Company, PO Box 1, 729 Prospect Avenue, Osceola, WI 54020-0001 USA

© Michael Green, 1995

MBI Publishing Company books are also available at discounts in bulk quantity for industrial or sales-promotional use. For details write to Special Sales Manager at Motorbooks International Wholesalers & Distributors, 729 Prospect Avenue, PO Box 1, Osceola, WI 54020-0001 USA.

Library of Congress Cataloging-in-Publication Data
Green, Michael
    Patton's tank drive, D-Day to victory / Michael Green.
        p. cm.
    Includes index.
    ISBN 0-7603-0163-8 (pbk.)
    1. Patton, George S. (George Smith), 1885-1945.
    2. World War, 1939-1945--Tank warfare. 3.
    World War, 1939-1945--United States. I. Title.
    D793.G74   1995
    940.54'1273--dc20   95-36435

On the front cover: Waiting for the order to move forward is a long column of Shermans. *Patton Museum* **Inset:** General George S. Patton. *Patton Museum*

On the back cover, top: An M5A1 light tank somewhere in Europe. *Patton Museum* ***Bottom:*** The M1A1 Combat Car pictured with General Patton was the vehicle he used while commanding part of the 2nd Armored Division during the large prewar maneuvers held in September 1941. This vehicle carries two sets of stars, on the front hull in the form of a pennant and on the front of the turret. The other pennant on the front hull is a divisional pennant. *Patton Museum*

Printed in the United States of America

★ ★ ★ ★

Contents

	Acknowledgments	4
	Introduction	5
CHAPTER ONE	**Patton's Return To Armor**	6
CHAPTER TWO	**Patton In North Africa**	19
CHAPTER THREE	**Patton Invades Sicily**	50
CHAPTER FOUR	**Patton Enters The War In France**	65
CHAPTER FIVE	**The Battle of the Bulge**	108
CHAPTER SIX	**Patton's March Across Germany**	124
CHAPTER SEVEN	**Patton's Postwar Thoughts**	144
	Bibliography	159
	Index	160

★ ★ ★ ★

Acknowledgments

Special thanks are due to the staff of the Patton Museum of Cavalry and Armor, Fort Knox, Kentucky, whose support and help made this book possible. Thanks are also due to the helpful staff of the Armor School Library at Fort Knox, Kentucky, and the United States Army Center for Military History located in Washington DC. Numerous other individuals and organizations such as the associations of the 1st, 2nd, 4th, 5th, and 6th Armored Divisions were kind enough to allow me to use both pictures and stories from their wartime service with Patton's armies.

★ ★ ★ ★

Introduction

The newspapers called him "Blood and Guts." His men in Africa called him "Gorgeous Georgie" after his distinctive way of dressing. The men of the Third Army simply called him "Georgie," his nickname from childhood. Whatever the nickname, George S. Patton Jr. represented a rarity in the US Army and, unique in the European-African-Middle Eastern theater; the cult of personality. To this day, while other World War II veterans identify with their division and often only to the regiment or battalion, men of the Third Army say, "I was with Patton."

Patton was a consummate actor, displaying many faces to suit the need of the moment. Most famous was what he called his "war face." A lifetime of study had convinced Patton that this should be his leadership style.

Martin Blumenson, Patton's biographer, wrote: "His toughness, his profanity, his bluster and braggadocio were appurtenances he assumed in order to inspire soldiers and, incidentally, himself. He cultivated the ferocious face because he believed that only he-men, as he often said, stimulated men to fight. Like Indian war paint, the hideous masks of primitive people, the rebel yell, the shout of paratroopers leaping from their planes, the fierce countenance helped men in battle disguise and overcome their fear of death."

This book in no way attempts to be a definitive history of Patton and his exploits throughout World War II. Space limitations prohibit that. Instead, your author has decided to give a broad overview of some of Patton's activities through World War II that concentrate on his armor formations and their vehicles and weapons. It was Patton's armored divisions and their tanks that spearheaded the Allied drive to the Rhine.

To give the reader an insight into Patton's mindset during World War II, many of his wartime messages and orders are included in the text.

As a preface to the book itself, a short note of explanation is due to some readers who may not be familiar with the American World War II chain of command. Patton was made a divisional commander (two-star general)

shortly before the United States entered World War II. An American Army division was, at the time, anywhere from 12,000 to 20,000 men. It was at the divisional-commander level of the US Army that tactical combat decisions were normally made. What roads the tanks would go down, how many tanks might be used in the attack, and what units would be used. Above this level of command, war normally consisted of pouring over large maps day after day. When a decision was finally made, it would then be relayed to the divisional-level field commanders, who would actually implement the big-picture decisions made by higher ranking officers.

When Patton took command of the I Armored Corps, which led the invasion of North Africa, he was then a corps commander (three stars), which meant he had up to four divisions under his command at any one time.

When Patton stepped ashore in France in July 1944, he was an army commander (three stars later promoted to four stars) in charge of four army corps, which themselves could consist of almost any number of divisions (normally ranging from two to six) in each corps. Also attached to each corps were a large number of supporting units ranging from artillery to independent tanks and tank-destroyer units.

All the various wartime American Army units, ranging from battalion level to divisional level and then all the way up to the corps level, were designed as interchangeable building blocks that could be moved around from one command level to another, depending on the mission they needed to fulfill.

Patton was commander of the US Third Army from July 1944 up to the end of the war in Europe in May 1945. Almost forty-three different US Army divisions served under his command at one time or another. Some divisions would serve under his command for only a few short weeks before being transfered to another army command. Other divisions, such as the 4th and 6th Armored Divisions, would serve under Patton's Third Army command during almost the entire European campaign.

CHAPTER ONE

PATTON'S RETURN TO ARMOR

On June 22, 1940, a broken and bewildered France accepted the humiliating terms of a German armistice. So rapid and so complete had been the impact of the Nazi Blitzkrieg that it was over before the world realized it had begun.

So entered the era of mobile tank warfare in World War II.

According to US Army Major General Adna R. Chaffee, father of the armor branch: "The important lesson in the French campaign is the use of an armored force as an independent army. This armored army supported by combat aviation made the main strategic and tactical effort of the German Field Forces. Its attack was made through an extremely rugged terrain zone using only the combined arms of its component elements."

The early success of German armor hurried the creation of America's own armor organization. A War Department order of 10, July 1940 created the Armored Force, consisting of the 1st and 2nd Armored Divisions and the 70th Tank Battalion. The Armored Force School and Replacement Center, now the US Army Armor School, was established October 1, 1940 at Fort Knox, Kentucky.

On May 14, 1940, Chaffee went before the American Congressional Subcommittee on Appropriations where he stated his impressions on why the French Army (considered to be the best in Europe prior to their defeat) failed to stop the German invasion of their country: "Even after the experiences of the Polish campaign the French had no concept of the unified tactical action of the combined arms grouped in the armored division 'nor of' the supreme importance of the role of combat aviation combined with the armored force." He also noted that prior to the present war the British "failed to evaluate properly the importance of the combined arms in armored units. Especially did they fail to appreci-

By the end of World War I, Patton's courage and leadership in combat had gotten him promoted to the rank of colonel in charge of a brigade of tanks. This studio shot taken at the end of the war shows him as a colonel. Despite Patton's hope for the creation of an independent tank corps, it was not going to happen. On June 2, 1920, the US Congress passed the National Defense Act, which abolished the tank corps as an independent arm and assigned all remaining tank units to the infantry branch. Patton himself, transferred back to the cavalry. *Patton Museum*

One of the better known pictures of Col. George S. Patton Jr. from World War I shows him posed in front of a French-built Renault light tank sometime somewhere in France in 1918. Patton was hand-picked by General "Blackjack" Pershing to both train and command two battalions of light tanks in late 1917. Since American factories never managed to produce any of its their own tank designs before World War I ended, American tankers were forced to make do with French light tanks or British-supplied heavy tanks. *Patton Museum*

ate the importance of specialist infantry and combat aviation support . . ."

Despite the fact that as late as June 1941 there were only sixty-six medium tanks in the US Army, visions of armored armies, corps, and divisions were being imagined by leaders such as Patton and Chaffee. General Chaffee defined the role of the armored division as "the conduct of highly mobile ground warfare, primarily offensive in character, by a self-sustaining unit of great power and mobility."

With the organization of armored divisions, the long envisioned team of combined arms was now in getting closer to re-ality. However, the original roles of the tank were still considered appropriate by many of the most important military leaders of the day. They saw tanks in only two basic roles: the first was the use of separate tank battalions that were organized and trained to support the infantry division; the second was the use of armored divisions that were organized for missions requiring independent action, using great mobility and firepower. In the battles for Poland and France, German armor divisions had performed the same two missions. It would take Patton to combine the two missions together in his Third Army in 1944–45.

The French-built Renault light tank used by Patton's soldiers weighed about seven tons and was powered by a four-cylinder water-cooled gasoline engine; that gave it a top speed of 5mph on level ground and 1.5mph while going cross-country. The vehicle's armor protection was only 16mm thick. This offered protection from only machine-gun fire or shell splinters. When one of Patton's light tanks ran into something more powerful, the results could be pretty serious for both the crew and vehicle. *Patton Museum*

Patton's Early Commands

In WW I, Patton had commanded the 344th Tank Battalion, one of the two battalions that provided the bulk of the officers and men for the 66th Armored Regiment, which was the only American tank unit to see combat in World War I.

Before the start of World War II, Patton was a colonel in the 2nd Armored Division. Patton's name was then placed by General Chaffee on a list of officers who he felt were suitable for promotion to brigadier general and for command of an armored brigade. While Patton's age (fifty-four) put him at a disadvantage against many younger and very promising colonels who were trying to fill the same position, Patton had always made a habit of cultivating friends in high places and was lucky enough at the time to find a good friend, Henry L. Stimson, appointed as the Secretary of War by President Franklin D. Roosevelt. This and the fact that the commander

For training purposes the French lent Patton twenty-two of their Renault light tanks. When his unit arrived at their new training base, Patton was forced to drive off all twenty-two of the tanks from their rail cars since nobody in his tank force had ever driven a tank before. Patton had received his training on these tanks at the French Army tank school prior to taking command of the American tank training school. The Renault light tank had a two-man crew and was armed with either a short-barreled 37mm cannon or an 8mm machine gun. *Patton Museum*

One month before the US Congress transferred control of all tank units to the infantry branch of the US Army, Patton wrote an article in the May 1920 issue of Infantry Journal in which he stated: "The tank is new and, for the fulfillment of its destiny, it must remain independent, not desiring or attempting to supplant infantry, cavalry, or artillery, it has no appetite to be absorbed by any of them. The tank corps grafted on infantry, cavalry, artillery, or engineers, will be like the third leg to a duck—worthless for control, for combat impotent." The vehicle pictured is an American-built copy of the French-designed light tanks commanded by Patton in World War I. *Patton Museum*

of the 2nd Armored Division at the time, General Charles Scott, was a long-time friend of Patton made him a shoe-in for the open slot as brigadier general in the 2nd Armored Division.

At that point in time, the 2nd Armored Division, was a miniature army built around a tank brigade, and was authorized 754 officers, 69 warrant officers, and 13,795 men, a total of 14,618 officers and men. Patton was placed in command of the 2nd Armored Brigade of the 2nd Armored Division.

With General Patton commanding the 2nd Armored Brigade, the remainder of the division formed a flexible support and supply echelon for the "iron fist." On September 18, 1940, Major General Charles Scott was appointed commander of the I Armored Corps, which consisted of the 1st and 2nd Armored Divisions. General Patton then assumed command of the 2nd Armored Division.

As a result of reports from observers of armored tactics on world battlefronts and in maneuvers, it was decided to reorganize the armored division into two combat commands, operating under control of the division commander but capable of acting independently, if necessary. The reorganization resulted in a reallocation of officers, men, and equipment within the division to bring about a more flexible tactical unit.

Under the new plan, the one armored regiment was inactivated, and its personnel and equipment were divided between the two remaining tank regiments, thereby giving the regiments two medium tank battalions and one light tank battalion each.

The division's armored field artillery regiment was considered too unwieldy tactically, and was inactivated. In its place was created the division artillery, consisting of division artillery headquarters and three armored field artillery

Pictured here in a prewar tanker's uniform, a sour-faced Patton is wearing a one-piece herringbone twill overall and a leather composition crash helmet with goggles. This prewar tanker's helmet featured a thick ring of padding around the head at brow level. By the time the US had entered World War II, a different version of the tanker's helmet had been issued. Neither version offered any ballistic protection for the wearer, but it did protect the head from contact with the unpadded interiors of tanks. Many tankers wore the outer steel shell of the standard M1 helmet over their leather composition helmets for added protection. *Patton Museum*

With the outbreak of the war in Europe in 1939, and the reforming of the Armored Branch Force under the command of General Adna Chaffee (considered the "Father of the Armored Branch Force"), Patton desperately sought ways of getting a command position in this newly formed force. It wasn't until his friend General Chaffee helped him get a post as a brigade commander in the newly formed 2nd Armored Division in July of 1940 that he realized his dream of returning to tanks. A smiling Patton on the left of this picture is sharing a moment of humor with another general officer on the right. *Patton Museum*

battalions—all identical in strength and organization.

Combat Command A and Combat Command B were created from division personnel as tactical subheadquarters of the division. In tactical situations, the composition of the two combat commands was to be dictated by the mission of the division. The reorganization permitted the division commander to provide two small armored divisions of equal strength and composition when he desired.

In addition to Combat Command A, Combat Command B, and the division artillery section, a fourth tactical headquarters, the division trains headquarters and headquarters company were created. Its tactical mission was to consolidate the service and supply units of the division.

Despite Patton's well-known and long association with tanks, it was General Adna Chaffee and General Daniel Van Voorhis (known as the "Grandfather of the Armored Force") who managed to preserve a US Army interest in tanks between the end of World War I and the beginning of World War II. Standing to the left of Patton with a cane in his hand is Henry L. Stimson, Secretary of War under President Roosevelt. Stimson is pictured here attending one of the 2nd Armored Division's prewar training exercises. *Patton Museum*

When Patton assumed command of a brigade of the 2nd Armored Division in July 1940, the American tank fleet was in pretty sad shape. What interest and money that was received from the US Congress had been spent on the development of light tanks. This was a trait shared by many of the world's tank-producing armies prior to World War II. Pictured are a trio of M1 Combat Cars (the cavalry's name for tanks until June 1940). *Patton Museum*

The specialist battalions within the division were also redesignated and remodeled internally, so they, too, could be split into two parts of equal or similar strength.

On January 19, 1942, Brigadier General Willis D. Crittenberger assumed command of the 2nd Armored Division, succeeding Major General Patton, who was then named commander of the I Armored Corps.

The very small ten-ton M1 Combat Car and other versions in the series had a four-man crew and were armed only with machine guns. One .30-caliber machine gun was mounted in the front hull and another .30-caliber machine gun mounted was alongside a .50-caliber machine gun in the vehicle's turret. Powered by an aircraft-type gasoline engine, the vehicles were very fast, but obsolete by the time America entered World War II. *Patton Museum*

The M1A1 Combat Car pictured with General Patton was the vehicle he used while commanding part of the 2nd Armored Division during the large prewar maneuvers held in September 1941. Always a showman, Patton wanted to make sure that everybody knew when he was around. This vehicle carries two sets of stars, on the front hull in the form of a pennant and on the front of the turret. The other pennant on the front hull is a divisional pennant. *Patton Museum*

Another tank in use with the US Army when Patton returned to the newly created Armored Force was the M2A2 series of light tanks. Based on the same basic chassis as the cavalry's combat cars, these vehicles had a four-man crew and were armed with three machine guns: one mounted in the front hull and two others, each mounted in a small one-man turret. While this multi-turret design looks strange now, most other tank-producing armies of the world had tried out this same design prior to the start of World War II. Neither the M1 Combat Cars series or the M2A2 series saw combat service in World War II. *Patton Museum*

LEFT
The only light tank in service with the US Army in 1940 that had anything mounted on it more powerful than machine guns was the M2A4 light tank, armed with a 37mm gun in a two-man turret. The basic vehicle chassis was the same as used on the Army's other light tanks. None saw combat with the US Army in World War II. *Patton Museum*

The standard infantry antitank weapon of the prewar US Army was the towed 37mm gun. Shown here in a posed picture taken during a training exercise is a ground-mounted 37mm gun and crew. It was this weapon that would be sent to North Africa in 1942. In combat the weapon did not stand up well. According to a wartime report, "This gun is useless as an anti-tank weapon and strongly recommended that it be discarded." *Patton Museum*

Between the end of World War I and the beginning of World War II, the US Army designed, tested, and employed a wide variety of civilian-modified scout cars. However, it wasn't until the mid-1930s that the US Army began looking at designing a more specialized reconnaissance vehicle from the ground up. The final result was the M3A1 Scout Car that came out in 1939, which saw widespread use during prewar training exercises. The vehicle's thin armor, combined with very poor cross-country mobility, limited its role to mostly secondary or non combat duties. *Patton Museum*

Another armored vehicle developed for the pre-World War II US Army was the M1 Armored Car. Developed during the early 1930s, less than a dozen would be built. Almost sixteen feet long, seven feet high, and six feet wide, the five-ton M1 could reach speeds up to 55mph. It was armed only with machine guns. The frame-mounted spare tires (one on each side) were designed to assist in cross-country running. The vehicle never saw service in World War II. *Patton Museum*

With World War II breaking out with the German invasion of Poland in September 1939, the US Army found itself ill-prepared to deal with the threat of war. To a great extent the US Army had been neglected ever since the end of World War I in 1919. To help reassure the American public in the late 1930s that America still had a powerful military force, many posed pictures of America's military forces were released. *Patton Museum*

When Patton took a command position in the newly formed 2nd Armored Division in July 1940, out of the roughly 400 tanks in the US Army inventory at that time, only eighteen M2 medium tanks could be really considered modern tanks when compared to the German tank fleet of the same period. The M2 medium tank and an improved model, the M2A1, were armed with a single turret-mounted 37mm gun and six hull-mounted .30-caliber machine guns. Never seeing combat, this vehicle was used only in training. Nevertheless, its design would be utilized later when its chassis would form the starting point for development of both the M3 and M4 medium tank series. *Patton Museum*

CHAPTER TWO

PATTON IN NORTH AFRICA

On November 8, 1942, American soldiers waded through the pounding surf of the French North African beaches in three widely separated areas to begin the largest amphibious operation ever attempted in military history. The invasion armada consisted of almost 900 ships, with a strong contingent of battleships, cruisers, aircraft carriers, and destroyers providing fire support for the troops as they landed on the enemy shores.

The decision to invade French North Africa, which consisted of the countries of Morocco, Algeria, and Tunisia, was made by President Roosevelt despite the fact that most of America's military leaders doubted the value of the invasion and the chances of its success. However, Roosevelt strongly believed that it was very important to give the American public a feeling that they were at war with Nazi Germany, as well as the Empire of Japan. Other reasons were to relieve pressure on the hard-pressed Soviet military, and to stop German power from spreading in the Middle East.

Overall command of the American forces used in the invasion of French North Africa was entrusted to General Dwight Eisenhower. It was Eisenhower who decided that Patton was the best man to command the main American landing force in the upcoming assault.

Eisenhower had known Patton from the time they were both junior officers in the American Army before World War I. Eisenhower's relationship with Patton could never really be called a friendship. They both were very aware of the each other's strong points and weaknesses and never missed any chance to criticize each other. This can be seen in their respective wartime writings. During World War II, Eisenhower always saw Patton as a valuable subordinate who was very good at

In a wartime report: 2nd Lieutenant Kenneth D. Warren, who served with Patton in North Africa, stated "Replacements need more training in arms. We have infantrymen who had never had any training in armored forces tactics, and armored infantry is a lot different from regular infantry." Lieutenant Warren went own on to say: "The enemy will shell you from his tanks and he's good with his mortars too. Recruits need general training, especially in how to place and use their weapons." Posing for the camera in this early war picture is a typical US Army infantryman armed with his trusty M1 Garand rifle. *Patton Museum*

When elements of Patton's 2nd Armored Division sailed in convoy toward the shores of French North Africa (an invasion code-named Operation Torch) in November 1942, there were two types of tanks being carried aboard the transport ships. One was the relatively new M3 medium tank, as pictured here. The M3 medium tank was based on the chassis of the prewar M2A2 medium tank. Besides being armed with a large number of machine guns, the vehicle was equipped with a hull-mounted 75mm cannon with a very limited field of fire. It also had a smaller turret armed with a 37mm cannon mounted on top of the vehicle's hull. *Patton Museum*

actions that required a high level of initiative and aggressiveness. Frequently, Eisenhower would call on Patton when he needed someone with those qualities.

Of the three task forces assembled to invade French North Africa, Patton's command was the largest, with 24,000 men and over 250 tanks of the 2nd Armored Division. Arrayed against Patton's invasion troops was a formidable collection of French coastal-defense batteries including: field artillery, anti-aircraft guns, and machine-gun-armed pillboxes. The most heavily defended position in French Morocco, where Patton's forces were to be landed, was the small seacoast town of Fedala, about twelve miles northeast of Casablanca. The city of Casablanca was also well protected by French-built defensive positions. In support of the city's ground defenses, the local French commander could call on the big guns of a French battleship moored in the city's harbor.

OPPOSITE PAGE TOP
In US Army service, the M3 series of medium tanks had a crew of seven. While over 6,000 models of the M3s were built between April 1941 and December 1942, the tank itself was built only as a stop-gap vehicle until production of the better-known M4 Sherman tank series could begin. The M3 medium tank was not a popular vehicle with its crews. It was too high at ten feet, three inches tall, and the limited field of fire from its hull-mounted 75mm gun made it difficult to maneuver in combat. Pictured is an unrestored M3 series medium tank owned by a private collector in California. *Michael Green*

As Pattons and his troops sailed across the Altantic towards French North Africa, he gave them a message to help explain their mission. It read: "We are now on our way to force a landing on the coast of North West Africa. We are to be congratulated because we have been chosen as the units of the Unit-

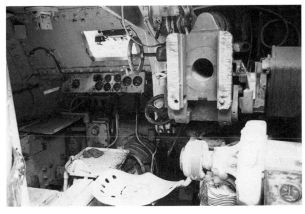

Pictured is the front hull interior of an early model M3 medium tank belonging to tank collector Jacques Littlefield. On the left of the picture can be seen the driver's control panel and his opened vision port. Just below the driver's control panel is the driver's seat, which was located on top of the vehicle's transmission. On either side of the transmission, under the driver's control panel, are the driver's two steering laterals. On the right of the picture is the breech end of the vehicle's 75mm gun, and below that, the gunner's seat. *Michael Green*

When it came time for Patton's 2nd Armored Division to land on the beaches of French North Africa in the early morning hours of November 8, 1942, it was only the M5 light tanks of the division that could be brought ashore since there were no specialized tank landing ships available at the time. The M3 medium tanks of the division would have to wait until a suitable French port could be captured before they could be unloaded from their make-shift transport ships. The M5 light tank had a four-man crew and was armed with only a 37mm cannon and two machine guns. *Patton Museum*

ed States Army to take a part in this great American effort.

"Our mission is threefold. First to capture a beach-head, second to capture the city of

Casablanca, third to move against the German wherever he may be and destroy him....
"We may be opposed by a limited number of

★ 21

The M5 light tanks of the 2nd Armored Division that landed in French North Africa in late 1942 were basically an improved model of the earlier US Army prewar light tank fleet. The biggest differences between the M5 light tank and its predecessors were the twin Cadillac V-8 gasoline engines and automatic transmission. Most of the earlier light tanks built in the US prior to the M5 were powered by aircraft-type radial engines and had manual transmissions. The M5 light tank pictured is being passed by an M3 Scout Car during a prewar training exercise. *Patton Museum*

Germans. It is not known whether the French Army [there were roughly 60,000 in North Africa] will contest our landing....When the great day of battle comes, remember your training and remember that speed and vigor of attack are the sure roads to success....During the first days and nights after you get ashore you must work unceasingly, regardless of sleep, regardless of food. A pint of sweat will save a gallon of blood.

"The eyes of the world are watching us....God is with us....We will surely win."

Patton's main landing would be launched on the beaches immediately east of the small Moroccan coastal town of Fedala. Other smaller landings under Patton's command would be conducted at Mehdia, about 50 miles north of Fedala, and at the port town of Safi, 150 miles south of Casablanca. Since the US Navy had no landing craft which could unload the thirty-two ton Sherman tank, Patton badly needed Fedala's port facilities to get medium tanks ashore and into battle. From Fedala, Patton's main goal of Casablanca—the captial of French Morocco—was only fourteen miles away.

As Patton's landing craft headed towards their beaches in the early morning darkness of November 8, 1942, they were spotted by French searchlights, which were quickly put out of action by US Navy gunfire. In the rough surf and darkness, a number of American soldiers, weighted down by their weapons and

ABOVE
Unlike earlier light tank designs employed by the US Army, which tended to be box-like in shape with their flat, face-hardened armor plates held together by thousands of rivets, the M5 light tank was built out of homogeneous steel armor plates that were welded together. The M5 had a highly sloped front hull plate that greatly increased the vehicle's ability to deflect enemy fire. The three US Army M5 light tanks pictured are taking part in a training exercise. *Patton Museum*

equipment, drowned in the strong undertow on the landing beaches. Due to the inexperience of the sailors manning the landing craft and the poor sea conditions, more than half of

RIGHT
This interior picture shows the driver's position on an American M5 light tank. Visible is the driver's seat at the bottom of the picture. In the middle of the picture is the driver's control panel. On either side of the control panel are the driver's steering levers, which pivoted from the top of the driver's compartment. The sloped front armor on the M5 light tank provided both the vehicle's driver and the bow gunner/co-driver's position a lot more room than found earlier light tank designs. *Patton Museum*

The only tank-versus-tank combat that took place during the invasion of French North Africa occurred when the military commanders of the Nazi-imposed Vichy French regime ordered a unit of French light tanks with supporting elements to counterattack the American forces. The French unit was quickly spotted by the Americans, who first sent dive bombers to attack them and followed with as much of their own armored forces as possible. The attacking French tanks were the two-man R-35 light tanks. The Hotchkiss R-35 light tank pictured is on display at the US Army Ordnance Museum. *Michael Green*

these vessels would be lost in the first day of the invasion.

French Army opposition to the landings at Fedala were confined to some half-hearted delaying actions which were pushed aside with ease by American soldiers. By the afternoon of the 8th, the French town of Fedala was in American control.

That same morning, as a landing craft was being prepared to take Patton and his staff ashore, a force of seven French Navy destroyers set out from the harbor of Casablanca to attack the American ships supporting the landings. The US Navy cruiser Augusta, which Patton was about to leave from, quickly accelerated to full speed to engage the French warships. Trapped onboard, Patton was witness to a full-scale naval battle. As the battle continued, more French warships and submarines entered the fray. Even the French coastal artillery guns located at Casablanca opened fire on the American ships. The French efforts at disrupting Patton's landings were beaten off by the US Navy with heavy French losses. While Patton no doubt enjoyed the show, his main interest was getting ashore to take charge of his forces. It wasn't until that afternoon that the US Navy was able to get him there.

Once ashore, Patton found to his dismay, that the rear-area support troops were much more concerned with digging their foxholes than unloading the equipment and supplies that the combat units would need to advance on Casablanca. Using every foul word in the English language, Patton spent the rest of the afternoon trying to sort out and organize his troops into a semblance of order. Darkness ended Patton's efforts to whip his men together on that first day on enemy shores. However, Patton resolved to return the next morning and bring or-

Seen here in a prewar parade in Paris, France, a large number of two-man R-35 light tanks are on the move. The French Army R-35 has a cast-armor hull and turret with its heaviest armor being about 1-1/2in thick on the front of the vehicle. Powered by a six-cylinder inline gasoline engine, the top speed of the vehicle was 23mph. The vehicle's turret-mounted armament consisted of a very short, low-velocity 37mm cannon. *Patton Museum*

LEFT
French tanks made contact with American forces on the afternoon of November 9, 1942. The American force was comprised of M5 light tanks, two M3 medium tanks, and some half-track–mounted tank destroyers. The battle began with the tank destroyers laying down a base of fire, while the American M5 light tanks attacked the French in an inverted wedge formation. The French tanks were no match for the American tanks, and fourteen of them were quickly destroyed. In short order the French forces hastily retreated. Pictured is a French R-35 light tank that has lost its turret in battle. *Patton Museum*

der into the chaos he found that day. The next morning, every soldier on the beach near Fedala found out just how mad Patton could get when riled. Patton went so far as to take command of individual units and tell them what they should be doing and how. Whatever Patton said must have had an effect on his men. By the afternoon of the 9th, the disorder from the day before had been replaced by a smooth flow of equipment and supplies onto the beaches.

Short of everything from tanks to radios, Patton's first few waves of assault troops had managed to advance about four miles towards Casablanca by the evening the 9th. French military aircraft attacked the leading elements of Patton's forces without inflicting much damage, and French Army opposition on the ground was weak. By the 10th of November, Patton's troops had reached the outskirts of Casablanca.

On November 11, 1942, the Vichy French government and its military leaders decided to sign an armistice with Patton after only three days of fighting. Patton was a great admirer of the French, as he had spent a great deal of time in France both as a youth and later as a soldier. With little political direction from General Eisenhower, Patton made a highly

RIGHT
Because of differences in opinion by the British and American governments on the future direction the war should be going, President Franklin Roosevelt decided to meet with Prime Minister Winston Churchill at the city of Casablanca, Morocco, in mid-January 1943. While there, Patton made arrangements for President Roosevelt to review up to 40,000 American soldiers that had taken part in the invasion of French North Africa. Pictured on the right, a very proud-looking Patton is standing beside the jeep in which Roosevelt rode while reviewing the assembled troops. *Patton Museum*

On the evening of the 10th, Patton decided to launch a full-scale attack on the city the next day. Despite being outnumbered by the French forces inside the city, Patton always felt that bold and determined action could make up for any shortage of numbers. Rather than attack in

criticized decision to allow the former Vichy French government and its military forces to continue to run that part of North Africa under American supervision. Pictured in a Dodge command car, Patton and a former Vichy French Army general are about to review a military parade. *Patton Museum*

darkness and risk repeating the same confusion among his troops seen on the beaches a few days before, Patton planned to begin his assault on the city at 7:30 A.M. The French military leaders inside the city could see the hand-

A junior officer serving under Patton's command stated in a wartime report: "As a platoon leader, I learned that you've just got to lead your men. When you get out in front, they'll follow you easily. If you're moving in sections, the platoon leader must go in the forward section. And what's almost as important is the fact that every man must know what's going on. You've got to take them into your confidence and explain the show to them. They'll always respond with better fighting." Pictured on top of an M3 medium tank is the vehicle's commander who had his own mini-turret armed with a .30-caliber machine gun. *Patton Museum*

writing on the wall and decided to approach Patton in the early morning darkness to negotiate an armistice. The French agreed to Patton's terms, and shortly before noon of the 11th, the French surrendered to Patton's forces. Total casualties for Pattons invasion of Morocco was no more then 400 Americans killed and another 700 wounded.

The French would later admit that it was the threat of hordes of American tanks overrunning Casablanca that was the main factor in bringing about their surrender.

The landings in North Africa were vitally important to Allied strategy and, in addition, were of inestimable value as "test runs" for fu-

ture invasions. Lessons learned under actual battle conditions, at the cost of men and materiel, were to prove valuable in later landings in Sicily and Italy, where similar waterborne attacks were to be carried out. After the surrender of the Vichy French government in North Africa, Patton set up his headquarters in Casablanca. Between mid-November 1942 and early 1943, Patton, under Eisenhower's overall direction, was the military commander of all of French Morocco.

While Patton remained in Casablanca biding his time for a combat command, most of the American forces in North Africa headed eastwards towards German-controlled Tunisia.

By capturing the Tunisian port cities of Bizerte and Tunis, the Allies could cut off the German forces in North Africa from their supply lines.

Unfortunately, the American and British plans to surround and destroy the German forces in Tunisia were hamstrung by a number of factors outside their control. The most important being the terrain. The terrain between the cities of Algiers and Tunis was extremely rugged, with high mountains and narrow valleys, which made it impassable for large armor formations.

What was left of the country's transportation system was either in ruins or didn't even exist. This made it very difficult for the Allies, since they were already short of supply trucks.

No mechanized military formation will last for long without a dependable source of supply, be it ammunition for its weapons or fuel for its armored vehicles. What roads that did exist in Tunisia were usually washed away by the heavy winter rains that plagued the country between late November and February of every year. This problem, as well as the lack of any suitable hard-surfaced airfield, meant that the advancing American and British troops would have to go up against the Germans without complete control of the air over the battlefields. The Germans, in contrast, had a number of all-weather airfields in eastern Tunisia and had the support of German aircraft based in Sicily, Sardinia, and southern Italy. In addition

One of Patton's tank commanders in North Africa stated in a wartime report: "It's a funny thing, being tank commander. You have got to run the crew, be stern, and show leadership. I had a new driver for an M3 medium tank. I told him to drive up a slope to a certain place and then stop. He got excited and went all the way up the hill. I told him to back up to the right place. He got excited again and went all the way back down the hill. He wouldn't listen to the inter-phone communication, so I hollered to the 37mm gunner to stop him, as I had my head out." Pictured is the driver of an M3 medium tank. *Patton Museum*

According to Lieutenant Colonel Hightower in a wartime report: "A reconnaissance of the field, if you are lucky enough to be able to make it, is the most important thing I can think of. In tank fighting nothing is more important than expert reconnaissance of your routes of advance and withdrawal. Several times both we and the Germans have moved up on what we thought was a good clear route only to find a dry wash, nine or ten feet high, blocking our way, causing us to withdraw." Shown is an M3 medium tank on the move. The small flag being waved by the tank commander is for giving orders to other tanks under conditions of radio silence. *Patton Museum*

to the German aircraft, there were several hundred Italian planes in these areas that could be thrown at the Allies.

The German military quickly built up its forces in Tunisia as soon as the American and British forces landed behind them in Morocco and Algeria in November 1942. By early January 1943, the German commander in Tunisia had amassed a force of 45,000 men—15,000 of which were Italians. By early February 1943, German commanders decided to launch an offensive operation against the somewhat green and untried soldiers of the American Army in eastern Tunisia. The Germans felt that given a strong drumming by combat experienced German troops, the American Army would be slow to recover, allowing them to consolidate their hold on Tunisia.

The Germans began their attack just before daylight on February 14, 1943, with strong division-sized armored units breaking through the

COMPARISON OF GERMAN
75-MM, 50-MM, AND 37-MM ANTITANK GUNS

A senior officer in Patton's command stated in a wartime report: "Sir, if we're going to get anywhere, we must put greater emphasis on good reconnaissance. I know of one instance where we went into battle not knowing what was there. We saw the enemy tanks go into Faid Pass and that night we had a dry run back into our concentration area. Next day when the attack came off we found the thing was a blind—the pass was covered with deadly antitank stuff. It plastered our one company that went in." From a wartime Army manual comes this illustration of three different antitank guns used in North Africa by the German Army.

forward positions of American Maj. Gen. Lloyd R. Fredendall's II Corps at Sidi Bou Zid. This was the opening act in the drama that would become best known as the Battle of Kasserine Pass. Within a period of seven days, the Germans managed to completely destroy six battalions of American troops and badly maul two others before withdrawing in good order.

Much of the blame for this large military disaster can be blamed on the inept handling of American forces by Maj. Gen. Fredendall, II Corps commander, and Maj. Gen. Orlando Ward, commander of the 1st Armored Division. Another problem that contributed to the terrible mauling was the fact that most American units had never fought as a team before. Tanks and infantry were expected to fight two separate, though related, battles. If a combined arms team of American tanks, infantry, artillery, and air sup-

port had been in place at Kasserine Pass, the US Army could have prevented the biggest route of their troops since the American Civil War.

With this disastrous defeat of II Corps, Eisenhower was forced to replace General Fredendall with General Patton on March 5, 1943, as commander of the II Corps.

With only eleven days before their next combat assignment, Patton quickly set about rebuilding American prestige by re-training, equipping, and organizing the four divisions that made up the American Army II Corps. Using all of his showmanship talents and outgoing personality, he tried to shape them into a fighting force equal to the demands of fighting a battle-tested enemy.

Patton's flair for the dramatics did not always make him popular with the officers and men that had to serve under him. From the wartime diary of the late Col. Henry Gardiner (a

A Staff Sergeant in the 1st Armored Division stated in a wartime report: "At Medjes-el-Bab [Tunisia] there was little or no reconnaissance. Our platoon of tanks was supposed to follow the right flank, and it was supposed to be protected by another platoon. We had no reconnaissance other than our own on foot. We walked the tanks in. We had no orders other than to await a tank attack. The following morning about 0900 hours, we lost two tanks to the 88mm guns. The first was the command tank. I went forward to get the crew and lost my tank by three 88mm gun hits." Pictured on display at the Patton Museum is an example of the dreaded German 88mm gun. *Michael Green*

much decorated tanker of the 1st Armored Division) comes this comment dated November 7, 1944: "Have seen a number of articles in the home magazines and papers about a general whom I recently met and who is now our big boss, most of which refer to him as 'Blood and Guts.' So far, as those of us who do the blood shedding are concerned, its 'Blood and Bull' and we don't like his movie newspaper complex." Patton was not an easy man to like. Throughout his military career, Patton's way of getting things done tended to make him as many ene-

BELOW
From a wartime report out of North Africa comes this humorous story: "Lt. McCracken of the 1st Armored Regiment told me, everyone thought Sgt. Jackson's buddy, Sgt. Hammer, was cracked when he remarked that he saw a building moving around. But it was a German gun position. They are very smart and use houses, sand dunes, or hay stacks as gun positions. The moving building turned out to be a vehicle with windows painted on representing windows of a house." Pictured is a line-up of M3 medium tanks with the 75mm hull-mounted cannon. *Patton Museum*

From a wartime report, a Lieutenant Colonel under Patton's command talks about German combat tactics: "Generally they [the Germans] try to suck you into an antitank gun trap. Their light tanks will bait you in by playing around just outside effective range. When you start after them, they turn tail and draw you in within range of their 88mm guns. First they open up on you with their guns in depth. Then when you try to flank them you find yourself under fire of carefully concealed guns at a shorter range. We've just got to learn to pick those guns up before closing in on them." Shown in this wartime picture is a captured German Army Mark II light tank. This type of vehicle was still being used by the German Army in Tunisia. *Michael Green*

mies as friends. It was his skill at making friends in high places that seemed to have carried him through the rough spots in his career.

While Patton did his best to instill some confidence in the men of II Corps, their very poor showing at the Battle of Kasserine Pass had convinced the British military commanders that the American officers and men of Patton's II Corps were not up to playing a major role in the upcoming campaign to force the Germans out of Tunisia.

On March 17, 1943, Patton's II Corps—which now consisted of three infantry divisions

BELOW
Lieutenant Thomas B. Rutledge of the 1st Armored Division in Tunisia stated in a wartime report: "One thing I learned was the next time we move up, before we close up on the objective, it is a good thing to look down on the ground in front of the objective and if you see anything that looks like the enemy or enemy guns, fire away at it with canister. We were so close that with keen observation, even two or three rounds or some machine gun fire would have downed many machine guns. I believe this would have saved us a lot of grief afterwards." On the move is an M3 medium tank. In combat, being seen first is often very dangerous. *Patton Museum*

An Army tank commander, who spent several months in North Africa, and saw heavy combat action stated in a wartime report: "When you are fired upon, if you have a good tank like an M4 medium tank (instead of an M3) you try to find out where the enemy is and fire even before you find a good position. Of course, it is best to get under cover as soon as you can. You should go from one firing position to another as a platoon [five tanks]. But at times, we must go on our own." Pictured is the vehicle commander of an M4 Sherman. *Patton Museum*

and the 1st Armored Division—was assigned the unrewarding task of drawing as many German soldiers to their advance across the Tunisia mountains as possible. The plan was to convince the Germans that Patton's II Corps was the main threat, when in reality, the British Army was to break through German defensive positions from the southern end of Tunisia. There they could enter the Tunisia coastal plain, where the German forces would no longer have the advantage of strong mountainous defensive positions.

By April 11, 1943, the British Army had pushed the remaining German and Italian forces into a small corner of Tunisia. It was at this point, as the British Army paused to prepare for the final assault on the enemy forces,

that Patton objected. Patton had learned that the British would only allow the American II Corps a minor role in the final campaign. He knew that the prestige of the American fighting man was on the line with the American public if they could not play a major role in the last battle of North Africa. Patton brought up this point to Eisenhower, who convinced the British to allow the American Army to share in the glory.

Before the final offensive action against the enemy was begun, Patton turned over the command of the II Corps to Gen. Omar Bradley. Patton was needed back in Morocco to help plan the invasion of Sicily, which would occur in about seven weeks.

A tank commander talks about American tank tactics in North Africa in a wartime report: "One must act on his own a great deal of the time. You can't wait to be told when to fire or where to fire. When you see something which you think is worth firing upon, take the chance.

The function of the officer is to keep the men together and tell them what is going on. The soldier has to use his individual judgment." Pictured is a company of M4 Sherman medium tanks in a training exercise in the United States. *Patton Museum*

RIGHT BOTTOM
A tank commander fighting with Patton forces in North Africa commented in a wartime report: "The gunnery instruction they gave us in the States was good. No Sir, I wouldn't change it. There's just one thing you must remember when you're fighting Germans. When you shoot at them they stop and try to kid you into thinking you knocked them out. Then when you turn your back on them, they open up again. Sir, we shoot until they stop and then keep shooting until they burn up." Typical of the type of German tank that the AmericanS were fighting in Tunisia is this Mark III tank on display at the British Army Tank Museum. *Paul Handel*

RIGHT TOP
"In tank fighting, one of the most important things is to keep your tank and its weapons in good condition," stated Lieutenant Norman of the 1st Armored Regiment fighting with Patton in North Africa. Lieutenant Norman went on in the same report to state: "You don't get a God damn thing done to the tank unless you do it yourself—and don't delay doing it. Bring lots of brushes to clean the guns." In this late-wartime picture, the crew of this M5A1 light tank is cleaning the barrel of their 37mm main gun. *Patton Museum*

LEFT
Staff Sergeant Wilbur R. White, who saw combat in North Africa, stated in a wartime report: "When under artillery fire, stay in your tank—it's better than any foxhole." Another North African veteran stated in the same report: "The tank is the best slit trench in the world when shells or bombs are falling. I feel safe in it and stick close to it at all times." Shown is an overhead shot of an M4 Sherman tank. Unless struck by a direct hit from a large artillery round, the Sherman was proof against both the blast and shell fragments from artillery barrages. *Patton Museum*

Another stop-gap weapon system that saw service in North Africa was a standard American-built half-track modified to mount a 105mm howitzer in a fixed forward firing position. The firing of the 105mm howitzer tended to crack the half-track's chassis, which had to be specially braced to withstand the gun's recoil. A little more than 300 were built before being replaced by the fully tracked M7 Priest. *Patton Museum*

Sergeant John T. Mahoney, who saw combat in North Africa, expressed his views on personal security by stating in a wartime report: "In a bombing attack, don't try to run too far from your half-track. Go about 20 or 30 yards and then hit the dirt." For those soldiers who decided to fire back at the attacking enemy planes, Lieutenant Colonel Hightower stated in a wartime report that the biggest problem was: "We find that our men are having trouble with their leads. You've got to shoot planes as you would ducks." The crew of this US Army M3 half-track are dismounting from their vehicle during a training exercise. *Patton Museum*

Private Blair H. Conard of the 6th Armored Infantry fighting in North Africa stated in a wartime report: "In a war there is no front. The enemy may come from the rear as the enemy tanks did to my company. We saw the tanks at the rear, but thought they were our own. One half hour later they moved up and shot the hell out of our half-tracks." Pictured on display at the British Army Tank Museum is a German Mark IV medium tank. Fitted with a high-velocity 75mm gun, this tank was a threat to American armored vehicles until the end of World War II. *Paul Handel*

RIGHT
Staff Sergeant Seaborn Duckett of the 6th Armored Infantry in North Africa stated in a wartime report: "We have had no opportunity to use the weapons on the half-tracks [machine guns] except for anti-aircraft fire." Sergeant John D. Mahoney who also saw combat in North Africa stated in the same report that even if the men on the half-tracks had targets to shoot at with their onboard machine guns "We have men who don't even know their nomenclature and functioning." A Colonel Ringsok was quoted in the same report as saying: "Many recruits have never even fired a .30- or .50-caliber machine gun or driven half-tracks." Pictured is an overhead shot looking into the rear passenger compartment of an American World War II half-track. *Patton Museum*

Sergeant John D. Mahoney stated in a wartime report: "The half-tracks have taken a beating, but they're OK." He also went on in the same report to say: "There should be a Coleman stove in each half-track to heat food. They would not give our position away like open gas flame does." Sergeant George Cleland stated in the same report that he felt: "The half-tracks carry enough ammunition." Shown in this prewar picture is an Army half-track slowly descending a steep slope during a training exercise. *Patton Museum*

Because of the high losses incurred by American light tanks during the fighting in Tunisia, General Omar Bradley commented in a wartime report: "Operations in Tunisia have indicated that the use of the light tank M3 and M5 in other than reconnaissance missions results in excessive losses." General Patton, as well as other most other high-ranking officers of the US Army involved in the fighting in Tunisia, concurred with this view. Shown at the annual living history show which the Patton Museum puts on every Fourth of July, is a US Army M3 light tank as used in Tunisia in 1942 and 1943. *Patton Museum*

A young American soldier, who fought in North Africa, wrote to his mother during World War II: "Our lives revolve around our half-track vehicles. When we first hit Africa, too many of us drove too fast, particularly across country. We broke springs, bent axles, got stuck under fire, lost our tools, and thought we were too tired to take care of our vehicles. Many men paid with their lives for this neglect. Now my squad never lets our vehicle out of its sight. We work on it at every opportunity; we steal to keep it going. We know that to keep this vehicle in shape and in operation is now a life-and-death matter to all of us." Pictured in a wartime training exercise is an Army half-track and crew. *Patton Museum*

Prior to the fighting in North Africa, the US Army felt that light tanks were to be considered the main striking forces of the newly formed armored divisions. In line with this train of thought, the armored divisions commanded by Patton in North Africa started off with many more light tanks in their inventory than medium tanks. This faith in the usefulness of light tanks was quickly ended when the increased effectiveness of German antitank guns and the restrictive Tunisian terrain showed light tanks to be death traps. Pictured near Maknassy, Tunisia, on April 8, 1943, is this M3 light tank belonging to the 1st Armored Division. *Patton Museum*

The fighting in North Africa also led many top American military leaders, including General Patton, to question the entire concept of separate tank-destroyer units. In late 1941 the US Army had set up a new military concept that envisioned specially trained and equipped tank-destroyer formations actively seeking out and attacking mass German tank formations.

Unfortunately, the concept was badly flawed from the start since German tanks almost always fought in combined-arms teams that included infantry, artillery, and air support. This prewar picture shows a US Army half-track towing a 37mm antitank gun. This weapon proved almost useless against German tanks in Tunisia. *Patton Museum*

LEFT
Since the American Tank Destroyer Command was formed in great haste, it was forced to make do with expedient weapon systems for training purposes until something better could be designed. Unfortunately, it was these weapons that saw combat in North Africa against seasoned German forces equipped with superior tanks and guns. Pictured is the M3 tank destroyer (later standardized as the M3A1), a standard M3 armored personnel carrier (half-track) modified to carry a low-velocity 75mm gun in a fixed forward firing position. *Patton Museum*

Despite some successful combat actions with the M3 tank destroyer against enemy tanks in North Africa during November 1942, in February 1943, during a German counteroffensive generally known as the battle of Kasserine Pass, American tank-destroyer units equipped with the M3 half-track armed with the 75mm gun took a serious beating. The main weakness of the American copy of the French 75mm gun was it low velocity (2,000 feet per second), resulting in a curved trajectory that made range estimation for the gun crews difficult against moving targets. *Patton Museum*

LEFT
For some American tank-destroyer units there was only one vehicle worse then the M3 with the French 75mm gun; the M6 (as pictured), armed only with a shielded 37mm gun mounted on an unarmored Dodge 3/4-ton truck. The M6 was supposed to have been only a training vehicle, but it was sent along with the first tank-destroyer units to arrive in North Africa. Having nothing but a thin armored shield for protection, it was suicide to engage German tanks with such a puny gun. One Army observer stated in a wartime report that "the sending of such a patently inadequate destroyer into combat can at best be termed a tragic mistake." *Patton Museum*

The arrival of the M10 tank destroyer late in the Tunisian campaign evened the playing field between German tanks and American tank destroyer units. Armed with a modified 3in naval gun in an open-topped armored turret and mounted on an M4 Sherman chassis, the M10 weighed about thirty tons and had a top speed of 30mph. It was not a perfect solution, but the commander of the tank-destroyer branch deemed it another expedient weapon system, and the troops themselves liked the vehicle. Captain A. R. Moore stated in a wartime report: "The M10s look good to me; all the boys who drive them swear by them. They use them hull down in defilade, nose over." *Patton Museum*

RIGHT
The German ground-mounted 88mm gun proved to be one of the deadliest surprises to American tankers in North Africa. According to Lieutenant Colonel L. V. Hightower: "Four 88mm guns, if dug in, are a match for any tank company. Once those 88mm guns start to bark, you can't pick them up in your tank. Attack them with infantry. Get the infantry out of the half-tracks. Don't take any thin-skinned vehicles with the tanks, they open on them the first thing. Don't take your assault guns or mortars with your tanks, because they will smash them in open country." Pictured on display at the US Army Ordnance Museum is this German 88mm gun fitted with a thin gun shield for the crew. *Michael Green*

In Tunisia, American tankers found that the German Mark IV medium tank (as shown) armed with the long-barreled, high-velocity 75mm gun was a much better antitank weapon than the 75mm gun found on their M4 Sherman. This didn't mean the German tanks always came out on top in battle. Staff Sergeant William Hagler described a combat encounter with German Mark IVs in a wartime report: "At Smitty's farm at Medjez-el-Bab on Dec. 10th, Germans packed mud on the turrets of their Mark IV tanks to make them look like our M4 tanks. Our own foot reconnaissance picked this up and we were ready for it. We waited until the Mark IVs were within 800 yards, then opened fire. We got five Mark IVs." *Patton Museum*

RIGHT
An Army sergeant stated in a wartime report: "What I've learned in Africa is that it is important to respect, not fear, the 88mm guns. You must keep in turret defilade. They can knock you out at 3,000 yards. I have also learned that tanks must have support. If we had air and infantry we could have done a good job. If the infantry had been ahead of us in the Pass, they could have helped quite a bit." Shown from the gunner's position is the interior of an M4 Sherman tank turret. Visible is the breech end of the Sherman's 75mm main gun. The large white-painted object around the gun is a body guard, designed to protect the turret crew when the main gun recoils back into the turret after being fired. *Michael Green*

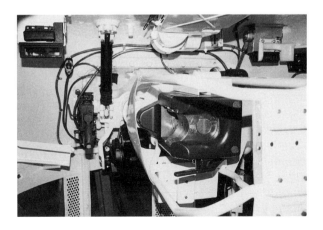

The scariest surprise for American tankers in North Africa was the introduction of the German Tiger I tank. In the World War II diary of Colonel H. E. Gardiner, 1st Armored Division, comes this description of his first encounter with a German Tiger I tank, the date is January 24, 1943: "The first recon, this time we made with a platoon of tanks. We had some interesting discoveries and signs on the ridge that had been vacated by the enemy. The most exciting of all was to find tank tracks of a size way beyond anything we had ever seen before. We had heard some G-2 reports to the effect that the Germans had a new tank in the theatre mounting an '88' known as the Mark VI. We now knew that we had engaged one and were very happy that it had decided to withdraw." Pictured is the crew of a Tiger I in Tunisia waiting for the call to action. *Frank Schulz*

LEFT
Sergeant Neal of I Company, 3rd Battalion, 1st Armored Regiment, describes a combat encounter with a Tiger I tank in a wartime report: "I am a platoon sergeant. In the action at Sidi bou Zid [Tunisia] I was the driver for the platoon leader. Suddenly we saw firing where G Company was. We fired back. We fired until we had orders to pull out and go back to Sidi bou Zid. Tanks kept coming. We pulled out and were met by a line of tanks from the southwest. That's where we lost four other tanks, including our tank. We were fired on by Mark VI tanks [Tigers] and 88mm guns. Our tank was hit in the turret. It listed and caught on fire. I believe it was a Mark VI tank which hit us." Pictured is a destroyed Tiger tank in Tunisia. *Patton Museum*

Pictured on display at the US Army Ordnance Museum located at Aberdeen Proving Ground, Maryland, is Tiger 112, which was abandoned by its German tank crew near Mateur, in northern Tunisia, sometime in May 1943. For further technical studies, the vehicle was shipped back to the United States, where it was dismantled, photographed, and evaluated by a variety of experts. At the end of the war it was placed on display. *Richard Cox*

LEFT
Throughout his long military career, Patton constantly sought to improve the military equipment then in use. Prior to America's entrance into World War II, Patton had tried to convince the US Army to adopt a tanker's uniform of his own design. While he was turned down on that idea and many others, he did use the power of his rank to modify his own personal command vehicles throughout World War II. During the few months he spent at the US Army's Desert Training Center, he had a half-track provided with overhead armor protection and a machine gun mounting at the front of the vehicle. *Patton Museum*

ABOVE AND RIGHT
When Patton took command of the II Corps in Tunisia in March of 1943, he used a slightly modified M3A1 Scout Car for getting around the battlefields. The biggest change made from a standard Army Scout Car was the addition of a large armored shield at the front of the vehicle driver's compartment. There was also an opening in this add-on armor for the mounting of a .50-caliber machine gun. As with any command vehicle for a general officer, the vehicle was equipped with a great deal of radio gear. Shown are two different views of Patton's M3A1 Scout Car in North Africa. *Patton Museum*

RIGHT
To command any successful combined-arms operation requires first-class communication equipment. Without such equipment it becomes almost impossible to control and coordinate the various elements that make up the combined-arms teams—which may include aircraft, artillery, infantry, and tanks. The German Army had always made heavy use of specialized command-and-control vehicles throughout World War II. The US Army also modified many of their vehicles into command-and-control vehicles. Pictured in this overhead shot of a US Army half-track is as much state-of-the-art radio gear AS they could jam into it. *Patton Museum*

BELOW
Located in the rear turret of this M4 Sherman tank is the typical FM radio found in most American tanks. The inherent advantages of FM radios in overcoming static and ignition interference and in giving a clear voice signal of sufficient quality and volume to be heard over the noise of tank operations made American tank radio equipment far superior to German tank radios, which only used AM radios. *Michael Green*

CHAPTER THREE

PATTON INVADES SICILY

Even before the last German troops surrendered in North Africa on May 6, 1943, the Allies were faced with the difficult decision of what to do next. American military leaders were convinced that all available forces should be returned to England in preperation for a cross-channel invasion of German-occupied France. The British, on the other hand, were positive that Allied resources were still not up to the job. The British had already learned a painful lesson about the consequences of a premature invasion of German-occupied France in Dieppe back in August 1942.

In order to placate Soviet demands for a second front, the British, using Canadian troops, had attempted a raid on the German-controlled French coastal town of Dieppe. The raid was almost a complete disaster, with heavy losses among the Canadian troops and the supporting British planes. The British therefore promised themselves that their next assault on German-occupied France would have enough strength that they would not repeat the Dieppe raid fiasco.

The British were very interested, at the time, in exploiting their victory in North Africa by continuing with other military operations in the Mediterranean—their ultimate goal being to force Italy out of the war. With Italy out of the war, the German military would be forced to stretch their limited resources even further. In the short run, this endeavor would help convince the Russians that the Western Allies were doing their part in fighting the war against Nazi Germany. In the long run, any military actions by the Allies in the Mediterranean would tie up German men and equipment, making them unable to support their

With a smile on his face in Sicily, Patton poses for the camera in a typically expressive posture. He is resting at least one hand on one of his two ivory-handled .45 Frontier model revolvers. Patton was an expert shot with his pistols. During the 1912 Olympic Games held near Stockholm, Sweden, Patton competed in the pentathlon which included pistol shooting. In 1916, as part of an American military force that entered Mexico in a quest to capture Pancho Villa, he was leading a squad of six men when they encountered three of Villa's bandits. In the ensuing gunfight he killed all three bandits with his own pistols. *Patton Museum*

When Patton left Tunisia in mid-April 1943, he turned over command of the II Corps to General Omar Bradley. Patton had been ordered by Eisenhower to start work on planning the invasion of Sicily, code-named Operation Husky. Shown in this picture is Patton on the left conferring with two officers from the 82nd Airborne and General Omar Bradley, who is in the middle of the picture. *Patton Museum*

RIGHT
Patton had serious doubts about the possible success of Operation Husky. He had proposed his own plan, which involved the American Seventh Army playing a central role in the invasion of Sicily. This plan was ignored, however, and a British plan was put into effect. Patton's Seventh Army was placed under the command of British General Alexander, with Eisenhower being technically in charge of the entire invasion as Supreme Commander. Pictured together at a military function in Sicily are Eisenhower on the left and Patton on the right. *Patton Museum*

comrades in France when the Allies actually went forward with their invasion plans.

To help push Italy out of the war, a mutual agreement was reached between the American and British government to invade the island of Sicily, which was controlled by the Italian military. About the size of the state of Massachusetts, the island consists mostly of a mass of rugged, steep mountains. Its major towns and cities were concentrated on the relatively flat coastal areas of the island. Sicily would be defended by four Italian field divisions, five Italian coastal divisions, and a number of German troops and air force personnel. Both the 15th and the Hermann Goering panzer divisions had been reformed from elements evacuated

Patton's plan to have his Seventh Army play an important role in the invasion of Sicily was basically squashed at the demand of the famous British General Sir Bernard L. Montgomery (better known to most by his nickname "Monty"). While Monty was considered one of Britain's top generals in World War II, Patton had little respect for Montgomery's style of leadership or how he conducted his military campaigns. Patton felt that Monty was too cautious in combat and would not take any calculated risks. Pictured is Monty in front of a large map showing Patton how the island of Sicily should be taken. *Patton Museum*

Patton, in his never-ending search to improve armored force mobility, had become an expert in planning amphibious landings. The invasion of Sicily by American troops under Patton was the prototype of other amphibious landings that followed, such as those at Southern Italy, Anzio, Normandy (D-Day), and Southern France. While Patton played no part in the invasions after Sicily, he was consulted on all of them, both officially and unofficially. Here he is pictured in a landing craft approaching the coast of Sicily on July 11, 1943. *Patton Museum*

from Tunisia. Altogether, the enemy strength was estimated at about 300,000 men.

To conquer Sicily, the Allies amassed a total of over 100,000 men, 1,800 artillery pieces, 600 tanks, and almost 14,000 transport vehicles. To move and support this mass of men and equipment from the shores of North Africa to the beaches of Sicily, the Allies amassed a fleet of almost 3,000 vessels, ranging from battleships to small landing craft.

Before the actual airborne assault on Sicily was launched on the night of July 10, 1943, Allied aircraft and naval units had already done their best to destroy enemy defensive positions, supplies, roads, bridges, and shipping.

The Allied troops to be used in the invasion of Sicily would be under the overall command of the Fifteenth Army Group, which consisted of the American Seventh Army, formerly the I Armored Corps under Lieutenant General Patton, and the British Eighth Army under Gen. Bernard Montgomery, plus the Canadian 1st Division. The entire campaign, including operations of the navies under Adm. Andrew Browne Cunningham and of the air forces under Air Marshal Arthur W. Tedder, was under the supreme command of Gen. Dwight Eisenhower.

Despite General Eisenhower being supreme commander of the Allied invasion of Sicily, the British still felt that the American soldiers of the Seventh Army didn't have the experience or backbone to play a major role in the conquest of Sicily. The prize of capturing Sicily would be given to the British Eighth Army, led by General Bernard Montgomery. The British Eighth Army, which was to land on the southeastern coast of Sicily, would constitute the right wing of the Allied landing. Their main goal was the Sicilian port city of Messina. By capturing Messina, the Allies could cut off the Germans on Sicily from their supplies and reinforcements from Italy. Patton's Seventh Army would be relegated to the minor role of protecting the British left flank during the upcoming campaign. Both Patton and Montgomery would be under the direct command of British General Harold Alexander. He in turn, would have the very difficult job of trying to control two very self-centered prima donnas who totally disliked each other.

On June 27, 1943, Patton took the time to draft a message to his soldiers that would be read to them once they were safely on their ships and headed towards Sicily. The message read: "Soldiers of the Seventh American Army: We are indeed honored in having been selected by General Eisenhower as the American component of this new and greater attack against the Axis. We are teamed with the justly famous British Eighth Army, which attacks to our right, and we have for the Army Group Commander that veteran and distinguished soldier, Sir Harold Alexander.

"In addition to the armies, our attack will be supported by the annihilating might of the Allied Navies and Air Forces.

It was obvious to Patton that an aggressive, mobile force with adequate firepower was of the utmost importance. This enabled a landing force to drive the enemy back a sufficient distance from the initial beachhead to allow emplacement of supporting artillery for the infantry. In Patton's view, tanks play a key part in a successful landing operation. Pictured is Patton surveying the small Sicilian beach town of Gela, where American troops under his command first came ashore on July 10, 1943. *Patton Museum*

"Owning to the necessity for secrecy, I am unable to put in writing the location of our impending battle. However, I hereby direct the officers who will read you this after you are at sea to tell you where you are going and why.

Patton believed that after an initial amphibious landing and the establishment of a beachhead, the landing force must be prepared to throw back enemy counterattacks. For Patton, this was an important role for tanks. In the landing of the 1st Infantry Division at Gela, Sicily, tanks of the 2nd Armored Division were crucial in effectively repelling the strong German counterattacks. Among the German tanks that attacked the American Forces were a small number of Tiger I tanks of the Hermann Goering Panzer Division. The Tiger I pictured is an early production model. *Frank Schulz*

"When we land we will meet German and Italian soldiers whom it is our honor and privilege to attack and destroy.

"Many of you have in your veins German and Italian blood, but remember that these ancestors of yours so loved freedom that they gave up home and country to cross the ocean in search of liberty. The ancestors of the people we shall kill lacked the courage to make such a sacrifice and remained as slaves.

"During the last year we Americans have met and defeated the best troops Germany, Italy, and Japan possess. Many of us have shared in these glorious victories. Those of you who have not been so fortunate, now have the opportunity to gain equal fame.

"In landing operations, retreat is impossible. To surrender is as ignoble as it is foolish. Due to our Air Force and our Navy the enemy is unable to evacuate prisoners. Therefore, our soldiers who are taken prisoners will remain to strave and run the risk of being bombed or shelled by their own comrades who will be unable to tell prisoners from the enemy.

"Above all else, remember that we as the attackers have the initiative. We know exactly what we are going to do, while the enemy is ignorant of our intentions and can only parry our blows. We must retain this tremendous advantage by always attacking, rapidly, ruthlessly, viciously, and without rest. However tired and hungry you may be, the enemy will be more tired and more hungry—keep punching! No man is beaten until he thinks he is. Our enemy knows that its cause is hopeless.

"The fact that we are operating in enemy country does not permit us to forget our tradition of respect for private property, non-

In Sicily, the battle against the terrain was very intense. From the volcanic heights of Mt. Etna to the hill-winding roads to Palermo, the Sicilian battleground was filled with rocky mountains and deep valleys. Over an extremely limited road net, the US Army advanced in spite of stubborn German rear guards, prepared defenses, mines, and demolitions used at every opportunity. Pictured is an M4 Sherman moving along a Sicilian mountain road. *Patton Museum*

The American bazooka had some success against German tanks in Sicily. According to one company commander, his men developed so much confidence in their bazookas and rifle grenades that "they like to stalk tanks at night. We fire at the tracks and stop the tanks and then we can finish them off. We often found prepared positions where tanks were dug-in defensive positions and were hard to knock out with artillery. Our men would sneak up on them and blast them out of action with grenades and bazookas at close range. It was like big game hunting on a grand scale." *Patton Museum*

combatants, and women. Civilians who have the stupidity to fight us we will kill. Those who remain passive will not be harmed but will be required to rigidly conform to such rules as we shall publish for their control and guidance.

"The glory of American arms, the honor of our country, the future of the whole world rests in your individual hands. See to it that you are worthy of this great trust.

"God is with us. We shall win."

Patton's part of the invasion of Sicily involved landing the forward elements of his Seventh Army, which consisted of three infantry divisions, along a seventy-mile stretch of Sicilian shore in three simultaneous seaborne assaults. At the same time, he would keep the 2nd Armored Division on board their transport ships as a floating reserve to be landed where needed. The center point of Patton's landings was the small Sicilian fishing town of Gela.

In a futile effort to slow down Patton's tanks in Sicily, the Germans planted thousands of antitank and antipersonnel mines. An American battalion commander in Sicily stated that "one engineer platoon attached to a battalion combat team cleared 400 mines from six different fields. They were so thick that I couldn't tell where one field began and another ended. We lost four vehicles and I had to take my column off the road entirely and go across country." Pictured taking aim on an enemy target is a US Army M10 Tank Destroyer armed with a 3in cannon. *Patton Museum*

Other than some sporadic resistance by Italian coastal artillery positions and a very rough surf which led to some problems in the actual landing, Patton's troops managed to get ashore without difficulty on the morning of July 10, 1943. Unknown to Patton, the Italian and German defenders of Sicily had guessed correctly that Allied forces would land on the beaches of Gela to capture both the town and local airfield.

The Italian commander of Sicily had hoped to counterattack Patton's beachhead position at Gela that same morning in conjuction with strong German armor units. Unfortunately for him, a breakdown in communications prevented the Italians from linking up with their German counterparts. The Italian Army commanders decided to go on the offensive themselves. As Italian tanks attempted to storm Gela, American naval gunfire entered into the fray and took a heavy toll of the attacking Italian tanks. Those tanks that survived the naval gunfire were hunted down by American soldiers armed with bazookas and hand grenades. A mass Italian infantry charge by 600 men was cut to pieces by American small arms fire. By that same afternoon the Italians gave up on their efforts to take Gela. At roughly the same time the dejected Italian ground units left the area, the German forces finally reached the battlefield.

In combination with heavy artillery support and an attack by German and Italian planes on Patton's troop ships, elements of the Hermann Goering Panzer Division, equipped with the Mark IV medium tank, tried their luck at pushing the Americans off their Sicilian beachhead. Like the earlier Italian assault, the German tanks were beaten back by American naval gunfire. The Germans attempted another tank attack, which included Tiger tanks, a little bit later that same afternoon. However that attack met the same fate as the others.

Patton remained aboard a US Navy ship as the fighting raged that first day. He was well aware that the Germans would be back in force the next day. He quickly ordered that the men and tanks of the 2nd Armored Division be brought ashore that night as well as the next morning. Also brought ashore that same night were a number of artillery pieces.

Under fire from German 88s, Patton landed on the beach at Gela on the morning of the IIth. As Patton had guessed, the Germans and Italians had already launched a series of aggressive counterattacks against Gela earlier that morning. This time the German and Italian troops had to face not only the naval gunfire offshore, but the tanks and artillery of Patton's Seventh Army.

Patton himself became part of battle when he called in of some the naval gunfire on the advancing German formations. At one point in the battle the German and American soldiers were so close that the naval gunfire support had to be called off. During the fighting, the 1st Infantry Division was counterattacked by elements of the Hermann Goering Panzer Division, consisting of thirty to forty tanks (Mark VI, Mark IV, and Mark IV Specials). These tanks managed to penetrate the 1st Division positions on the plain northeast of Gela. A single platoon of the 67th Armored Regiment, assisted by artillery crews firing their cannons over open sights at the advancing German tanks, successfully repulsed the attack; destroying fourteen enemy tanks in the process.

Checking up on the progress of his troops in the battle for Sicily, Patton poses for the camera next to Brigadier General Theodore Roosevelt. General Roosevelt was the assistant commander of the 1st Infantry Division under Major General Terry de la Mar Allen. Both generals, Allen and Roosevelt, were extroverts and showmen of the Patton school of leadership. General Roosevelt would die of a heart attack shortly after the invasion of France in June 1944. *Patton Museum*

Firing at point-blank ranges, one of the American Sherman tanks involved in that engagement was credited with the destruction of three Mark VI Tiger tanks, as well as a German personnel carrier and an ammunition truck.

On the road to Palermo, Sicily, this American half-track (armed with a 75mm pack howitzer) is making its way through a small Sicilian town. When the Germans retreated through these towns and villages, they would often blow up buildings on both sides of the main road to block it and slow down the advancing American forces. The half-track variant pictured would later be replaced in field use by a full-tracked chassis based on the M5 light tank. *Patton Museum*

Meanwhile, almost continual bombing and strafing attacks were directed at Allied ships lying off Gela. Several ships and craft were damaged by near misses. One cargo ship, assigned to the 2nd Armored Division, received

By July 22, 1943, elements of the 2nd Armored Division, in conjunction with the 3rd Infantry Division, were racing toward the Sicilian port city of Palermo. Both the Italian military commanders and the civil leaders saw little hope in stopping Patton's Seventh Army. Wisely, they decided to surrender late in the afternoon of July 22. For a cost of only fifty-seven American soldiers killed and 170 wounded, Patton's troops took 53,000 Italian uniformed personnel and all of Western Sicily. Pictured are Italian troops being marched out of Palermo by American soldiers. *Patton Museum*

a direct hit from an enemy dive-bomber and burned. The cargo and vehicle load were a complete loss, except for a few landing craft unloaded prior to the attack.

By the end of that same day, the German and Italian attackers were forced to retreat from the battlefield leaving dozens of their burning tanks behind as a reminder of the battle's ferocity. The threat to Patton's beachhead at Gela was gone. The enemy would never make another attempt to force the Allies off the island of Sicily.

Once the beaches were secure, Patton's Seventh Army pushed further into Sicily. The tanks of the 2nd Armored Division had been split up into a number of smaller units so they could assist the American infantry divisions in the capture of a number of small Sicilian towns and villages. By mid-July 1943, over a quarter of Sicily was in Allied hands. At this point, Patton gathered all the different elements of the 2nd Armored back together into a division-sized formation. His plan was to throw this armored force at the other side of the island to capture the important Sicilian port city of Palermo.

The area around Palermo was defended by a number of German units and a mixed bag of second-rate Italian forces with little or no heart left to fight. Both the German and Italian military commanders already knew that the Allies had already won the battle for Sicily. Their only task was to delay the Allies as long as possible. The German soldiers on Sicily took this job a lot more seriously then the typical Italian soldier.

By July 20, 1943, the entire 2nd Armored Division was in an assembly area ready to go. To beef up the division, Patton attached additional engineer and artillery units. On July 21, in its advance toward the western part of Sicily, the 2nd Armored Division reached the Belice River. Castelvetrano was captured by the 82nd Airborne Division, which then continued its attacks toward Marsela, securing the left flank and rear of the 2nd Armored Division; which then turned north toward Palermo. The 2nd Armored Division launched its attack on Palermo at 6:00 A.M. on the morning of July 22. Combat Command A led the advance, with Combat Command B following by bounds. Combat Command A met strong resistance in each defile along its route. Antitank guns, manned by Germans, and well-emplaced machine guns manned by Italian infantry, were or-

Despite a lack of training and decent equipment, many Italian military units on Sicily fought bravely against the overwhelming American military superiority in both materiel and firepower. Of the roughly 200,000 Italian military personnel on Sicily when Patton's Seventh Army landed, over half were coastal defense units made up of older men with little equipment and poor leadership. Of the four Italian infantry divisions on Sicily, only one was up to full strength and had all the equipment it was suppose to have. Pictured is Patton in Sicily watching Italian prisoners of war march past. *Patton Museum*

ganized into a series of strong points, each one of which had to be surrounded and reduced by tanks and artillery before the advance could continue over the difficult route. At a pass four miles northeast of San Guisseppe, advance elements of the division met determined resistance, organized in depth, with large numbers of antitank guns up to 88mm in size. These guns were well-emplaced in the sides of the narrow pass and were cleverly camouflaged. Dismounted patrols, covered by tank and artillery fire, were successful in flanking the enemy positions, and resistance on the drive to Palermo was overcome. Combat Command A was ordered to halt on a corps' phase line just short of the city; where it remained until 6:00 P.M. that afternoon, when its first elements entered the city without opposition.

Combat Command B, moving northwest from Camporeale, ran into heavy German resistance. Its progress was further delayed by blown-out roads, tank traps, mines, and road blocks, but by 11:00 A.M. on the morning of July 23, the western outskirts of Palermo were reached and all resistance overcome.

By July 23, the city was occupied by both combat commands. Guards were placed on all docks, banks, utilities, and important buildings as a precaution against looting and sabotage.

On July 24 and 25, the task of guarding and patrolling Palermo was turned over to the 3rd Infantry Division, and all elements of the 2nd Armored Division assembled northwest of the city.

In an August 1, 1943, message to his troops, Patton congratulated them on their conduct during the campaign: "Soldiers of the Seventh Army and XII Air Support Command: Landed and supported by the navy and air force, you have, during twenty-one days of ceaseless battles and unremitted toil, killed and captured more than 87,000-enemy soldiers, you have captured or destroyed 361 cannons, 172 tanks, 928 trucks, and 190 airplanes—you are magnificent soldiers! General

Italian tanks had a reputation for being unreliable, underarmored, and undergunned throughout the fighting in North Africa. To increase the antitank ability of Italian tank units, the Italians took their excellent 90mm anti-aircraft gun and mounted it on the chassis of their standard medium tank. Only thirty were ever built, but they did account for some American tanks in the battle for Sicily. Known as the Semoventi DA 90/53 self-propelled gun, the example pictured is on display at the US Army Ordnance Museum. *Michael Green*

Eisenhower, the Commander-in-Chief, and General Alexander, the Army Group Commander, have both expressed pride and satisfaction in your efforts.

"Now in conjuction with the British Eighth Army you are closing in for the kill. Your relentless offensive will continue to be irresistible. The end is certain and is very near. Messina is our next stop!"

Following the capture of Palermo, Major General Alvin C. Gillem, Jr., commanding general of the American Army's Armored Command, was interviewed in the United States upon his return from Sicily. He had just completed a six-week tour of European battlefields and his comments were published in the *Armored Force News* of August 9, 1943, as follows: "I found that armored force soldiers were meeting expectations. They were tough, they were trained, and they were efficient. It made me proud indeed to be wearing the same insignia that the men of

the Armored Command overseas had on their overalls."

General Gillem went on to say: "The tank today is just as important a weapon as it was in 1940. Throughout the Sicilian campaign the tanks have contributed to the success obtained. The operations there have stressed mobility and firepower. The tank has fitted admirably into the picture. Its characteristics have been exploited by General George S. Patton, Jr. He has used the tanks ahead of or behind the infantry, depending upon the situation.

"The capture of Palermo furnished a perfect example of the use of a large armored unit in battle. During the first week of the operation, this armored unit was held in reserve. Infantry divisions on the flank were ordered to breach the defenses of one of the Sicilian valleys running north from the southern coast. The Armored Division was on a six-hour alert.

"When the opportunity presented itself, the Corps Commander shot the Division through the hole, turned it north into the valley and Palermo was captured almost per schedule. The speed and force of this one blow assisted materially to knock out all Axis defenses in the western half of the island.

"Up to the time I departed from Sicily, the total box score of American tanks versus Axis tanks, read 21 American tanks lost and 89 Axis tanks lost.

"A great deal of credit for the success of the campaign was due to the efficiency in the handling of supplies, fuel, and ammunition. Working with a very limited number of vehicles, supply and service units of the Division kept a steady flow of food, fuel, and materiel to forward echelon troops, despite constant attacks by enemy aircraft, over extended supply lines, and hazardous and unsatisfactory road conditions."

Unlike the fast-moving American Seventh Army, the British Eighth Army, under the command of Patton's arch rival Montgomery, had been stopped dead in their tracks by stiff German resistance along the east-coast roads of Sicily. General Montogomery's mission was to use his Eighth Army to capture the important Sicilian port city of Messina. The port of Messina was the number one goal of the Allies' entire Sicilian campaign since it was located only three miles away from the Italian mainland. Once Messina was in Allied hands, they could use it as a springboard to invade Italy itself. The Germans were well aware of this fact and had done everything possible to slow down the Eighth Army's advance. By doing this, the Germans could build up their military strength in Italy, and, at the same time, withdraw as many of their soldiers back into Italy to avoid capture on Sicily.

Much to Montgromery's dismay he was forced to admit to General Alexander (his boss and Patton's) that his Eighth Army could not break through the German positions to capture

Even before the invasion of Sicily began, Allied airpower had done much to destroy the morale of both the Italian military and even more so the Sicilian people. The German general staff and even Hitler saw the battle for Sicily as only a delaying action. The Allied military and political leaders who had approved the conquest of Sicily had hoped it would lead to the surrender of Italy. This was not to be. Pictured is Patton in his Dodge command car passing through a badly damaged Sicilian city. *Patton Museum*

★ 61

It was Patton's willingness to conduct amphibious end runs around German defensive positions during his time in Sicily that led him to beat British General Sir Bernard L. Montgomery into the important Sicilian port city of Messina, thereby ending the battle for Sicily. Pictured in the rear of his Dodge command car, Patton takes the time to talk to an American soldier on the way to Messina. *Patton Museum*

Messina. General Alexander then ordered Patton's Seventh Army, which had just captured Palermo, to attack in full force along the north-coast roads to Messina. No longer would the American Seventh Army play only a supporting role in the conquest of Sicily. It would be on equal footing with the British Eighth Army. It was Patton's hope that his men could not only relieve the pressure on Montgomery's stalled offensive, but could capture Messina before the British could even get there. If course, it also meant that Patton would claim all the fame and glory of winning the city and ending the campaign for Sicily.

At the same time the Allied armies were planning their final assault on Messina, the Italians did what the British military leaders had hoped for and decided to leave the war by kicking Mussolini and his Fascist government out of power on July 25, 1943. A badly enraged Hitler had the German Army quickly disarm the Italian military forces before they could be turned on them. Hilter also ordered that German troops be withdrawn from Sicily as soon as possible.

Patton's strong wish to quickly capture Messina was not to be. His Seventh Army ran head-on into the same types of strong German defensive positions that had stalled Montogomery's forces. Patton could not stand for any delays in his drive to take Messina. In an attempt to get around the enemy positions he tried to turn them by launching three small amphibious landings behind German lines. Unfortunately, the German soldiers facing Patton's force couldn't be forced out of their positions no matter what he tried. As casualties mounted among Patton's troops, he also began to fall under the mounting criticism of fellow officers who strongly objected to his conduct of the campaign. Things got so tense between Patton and his subordinate commanders that he was forced to relieve the commander and assistant commander of the Ist Infantry Division for not carrying out his orders correctly.

It was at this same time that a very unhappy Patton did something incredibly stupid that almost cost him his career in the Army, as well as the leadership of the American Army in the upcoming invasion of Nazi-held France. On two separate occasions during the month of August, while Patton was visiting his wounded troops at local evacuation hospitals on Sicily, he let his emotions get the best of his common sense. In both cases he found American soldiers residing in these hospitals that had no obvious battle wounds. Overlooking the fact that these men could have been there for any number of other reasons, Patton did the unthinkable and slapped his soldiers across the face and called them cowards. Patton saw nothing wrong in slapping his soldiers, he actually thought he was helping the men. Patton sent out a very cold and heartless memorandum to his senior commanders about the first incident, it read: "It has come to my attention that a very small number of soldiers are going to the hospital on the pretext that they are nervously incapable of combat. Such men are cowards, and bring discredit on the Army and disgrace to their comrades who they heartlessly leave to endure the danger of a battle while they themselves use the hospital as a means of escaping.

"You will take measures to see that such cases are not sent to the hospital, but are dealt with in their units.

"Those who are not willing to fight will be tried by Court-Martial for Cowardice in the face of the enemy."

Patton was lucky, word didn't get out on this first incident. Patton's luck ran out, however, on the morning of August 10. While making a quick visit to another evacuation hospital, he came upon a soldier suffering from shell shock, a more modern term is mental breakdown; he once again lost control and started to yell at the man. From the official US Army history of World War II comes a description of the event: "Patton began to rave and rant; 'Your nerves, Hell, you are just a goddamned coward, you yellow son of bitch.' At this point, Colonel Currier and two other medical officers entered the receiving tent in time to hear Patton yell at the man: 'You're a disgrace to the Army and you're going back to the front to fight, although that's too good for you. You ought to be lined up against a wall and shot. In fact, I ought to shoot you myself right now, god damn you.' With this Patton reached for his pistol, pulled it from its holster and waved it in the soldier's face. Then as the man sat quivering on his cot, Patton struck him sharply across the face with his free hand and continued to shout imprecations. Spotting Colonel Currier, Patton shouted: 'I want you to get this man out of here right away. I won't have these other brave boys seeing such a bastard babied.'

"Reholstering his pistol, Patton started to leave the tent, but turned suddenly and saw that the soldier was openly crying. Rushing back to him, Patton again hit the man, this time with such force that the helmet liner he had been wearing was knocked off and rolled outside the tent. This was enough for Colonel Currier who placed himself between Patton and the soldier. Patton turned and strode out of the tent. As he left the hospital, Patton said to Colonel Currier: 'I meant what I said about getting that coward out of here. I won't have these cowardly bastards hanging around our hospitals. We'll probably have to shoot them sometime anyway, or we'll raise a breed of morons.'"

Word quickly spread about Patton's vicious assault on the defenseless soldier in the evacuation hospital. By August 16th, Eisen-

Patton and Montgomery, at the end of the campaign in Sicily, are about to review a large Allied military parade. There was very little love lost between these two famous Allied military leaders. Despite orders from Eisenhower to let the British have the honor of taking Sicily, Patton felt very strongly that American military prestige was at stake during the Battle of Sicily and made sure the US Army would show up the British Army and Montgomery. *Patton Museum*

hower had reports on his desk about both incidents. Patton was ordered to make a public apology to all those who had been involved in the incident. He was also forced to visit every division of the Seventh Army and explain his actions.

The civilian press reporters assigned to cover the war in that part of the world decided among themselves not to spread the story to the United States out of fear that the American public would demand Patton's court martial. Despite their best efforts to contain the story, the American public found out. As expected, there was an uproar that called for Patton's resignation. Despite the outcry at Patton's actions, Eisenhower decided that Patton was too valuable to the war effort to be relieved of his duties. While this was good news for Patton, Eisenhower also resolved to himself that Patton would never again be given command over anything larger than an Army Command. Instead of Patton, Gen. Omar Bradley would go on to the job of commanding the American 1st Army in the invasion of Western Europe. Patton, who had been Bradley's boss for most of the war so far, would now be one of Bradley's subordinates for the rest of World War II.

While all this was going on, Patton and his Seventh Army finally managed to break through German lines to seize the port city of Messina on August 17, 1943, just a few minutes before Montgomery's Eighth Army entered the city. With this event, the battle for Sicily was over. Patton wrote a message to his troops dated August 22 in which he stated: "Soldiers of the Seventh Army: Born at sea, baptized in blood, and crowned with victory, in the course of thirty-eight days of incessant battle and un-ceasing labor, you have added a glorious chapter to the history of war.

"Pitted against the best the Germans and Italians could offer, you have been unfailingly successful. The rapidity of your dash, which culminated in the capture of Palermo, was equalled by the dogged tenacity which you stormed Troina and captured Messina.

"Every man in the Army deserves equal credit. The enduring valor of the Infantry and the impetuous ferocity of the tanks were matched by the tireless clamor of our destroying guns.

"The Engineers performed prodigies in the construction and maintenance of impossible roads over impassable country. The Services of Maintenance and Supply performed a miracle. The Signal Corps laid over 10,000 miles of wire, and the Medical Department evacuated and cared for our sick and wounded.

"On all occasions the Navy has given generous and gallant support. Throughout the operation, our Air has kept the sky clear and tirelessly supported the operation of the ground troops.

"As a result of this combined effort, you have killed or captured 113,350 enemy troops. You have destroyed 265 of his tanks, 2,324 vehicles, and 1,162 large guns, and, in addition, have collected a mass of military booty running into hundreds of tons.

"But your victory has a significance above and beyond its physical aspect—you have destroyed the prestige of the enemy.

"The President of the United States, the Secretary of War, the Chief of Staff, General Eisenhower, General Alexander, General Montgomery, have all congratulated you.

"Your fame shall never die."

CHAPTER FOUR

PATTON ENTERS THE WAR IN FRANCE

Having barely survived being sacked by Eisenhower for the slapping incident in Sicily, Patton would remain in Sicily until early January 1944 as commander of a paper army that no longer had any soldiers in it. Patton justly felt that the war would pass him by as he rotted away in the backwaters of Sicily. As heavy fighting raged in Italy between the American and German Armies, Patton's only role was as a historical tour guide for anybody he could talk into going with him on his Sicilian field trips. It wasn't until December 1944 that Patton got a chance to leave Sicily for a brief period.

Knowing that the German high command considered Patton one of the Allies most dangerous and aggressive generals, his British superiors decided to use him as a decoy to draw enemy attention away from their other on-going military operations. By sending him on various field trips around the Mediterranean, it was hoped that this would confuse German intelligence agencies as to what the Allies might be planning to do next.

Finally on January 22, 1945, Patton got the orders he was so desperately looking for. He was being called to England to play an important part in what would be the world's largest amphibious invasion.

On June 6, 1944 (D-Day), Allied forces had landed on the European continent with the mission of occupying Nazi Germany and de-

The American armored division that spent more time under Patton's Third Army command during World War II than any other, was the famous 4th Armored Division. Unlike other American armored divisions that had been given nicknames, the 4th had none. Major General John Shirley Wood, the division's commander, decided that: "The 4th Armored Division will have no nickname, they shall be known by their deeds alone." Pictured is a cast-hull Sherman. *Patton Museum*

stroying its armed forces. By the end of June, Allied commanders began to realize that their original estimates for their rate of advance into the interior of France were overly optimistic. In the British sector, units under the overall command of Patton's old friend General Bernard Montgomery were still stalled in front of the French city of Caen, which had been an objective planned for capture on the very first day of the invasion. Likewise, the Americans of the US First Army, commanded by Lt. Gen. Omar N. Bradley, found themselves behind

General John Shirley Wood was described by the eminent British military historian Liddell Hart as: "The Rommel of the American armored forces . . . one of the most dynamic commanders of armor in World War II and the first in the Allied Armies to demonstrate in Europe the essence of the art and tempo of handling a mobile force." Many American military leaders stated that General Wood frequently "out-Pattoned" Patton. On display at the Patton Museum is this M4A3 Sherman of the 4th Armored Division. *Patton Museum*

schedule and engaged in a grueling war of attrition with the German Army.

Even though the Allied landing was well underway in Normandy, General Dwight Eisenhower and the other Allied leaders sought to continue the deception that the Normandy landing was just a decoy to lure German troops away from the "real" landing site, which Adolph Hitler and many German military leaders were still convinced would occur at Pais-de-Calais, the closest point between England and France. To enhance the deception, Eisenhower forbade any publicity on Patton's entrance into the battle for France. The Germans were still being tricked into keeping a considerable number of their Fifteenth Army forces immobile because they were expecting

that Patton would land at Calais with the bulk of the Allied armies. They could understand his unexplained absence only as signifying that another Allied invasion of France and western Europe would take place in the very near future. The Germans knew that Patton had more combat experience than Bradley; they were conscious that he outranked Bradley in grade. Respecting Patton as a dangerous opponent, they logically expected the Allies to use him to head the main US forces in western Europe, which evidently had not yet appeared.

The Battle of Brittany

On July 6, 1944, General George Patton established his headquarters in the Normandy area of France. Under his command were four

The first elements of the 4th Armored Division landed on D-Day, June 6, 1944. However, it wasn't until July 14, 1944, that the entire division's inventory of men and equipment managed to arrive in France. They then headed southwest to aid in the breakout of American troops in the heart of France. General Wood's orders to his troops were, "This division will attack and attack. If the order is ever given to fall back, it will not come from me." A heavily camouflaged Sherman under fire somewhere in France. *Patton Museum*

corps, the VIII, XII, XV, and XX. When the Third Army finally became operational on August 1, 1944, Patton had three immediate objectives: to drive south and southwest from the French town of Avranches, to secure the area around the French cities of Rennes and Fougeres, and then to wheel westward to capture the French peninsula of Brittany and open the Breton ports to Allied shipping.

The Third Army under Patton would arrived on the scene in the midst of an ever-changing situation. By taking command of the VIII Corps, which by August 1, 1944, was rapidly approaching Brittany, Patton had assumed control of an ongoing campaign. Behind his front-line positions, the XV Corps headquarters, which had arrived in France on July 15, and the XX Corps headquarters, which had arrived on July 24, were also ready for action. The XII Corps headquarters, which was in control of the movement of Third Army units from England to France and pro-

cessing them from the original landing beaches forward, reached France in part on July 29, the remainder on August 7.

Long before Patton was landed in France to take command of the Third Army, Eisenhower, in conjunction with other top Allied military leaders, had already decided that the Brittany peninsula would be Third Army's number-one goal. The general idea was that the Third Army would be expected to begin their assault on Brittany sometime between two weeks and two months after the D-Day landing was complete. In Normandy since the early days of July, the commanders and staff of the Third Army despaired of performing within the original Allied time limits. Suddenly, less than a week before the planned limit would expire, they were ordered to take Brittany.

The French peninsula of Brittany was very important to the American Army and the other Allies because of its seaports: St. Malo, less than fifty miles west of Avranches; Brest, on

Sergeant Carl C. Cook, a tanker in Patton's Army, stated the following in his unit's history: "The darkest moment of my career in the Army came at our entrance into combat. I never realized that we were in combat until we lost our first man. I had seen German prisoners, German dead, American prisoners, and American dead, but they were not known to me. When I saw one of the tankers that I had known ever since basic training lying dead, that was my darkest moment. That's when I first realized what war really was." Pictured are the crewmen of a 4th Armored Division tank. *Patton Museum*

the western extremity of the peninsula; Lorient and St. Nazaire, along the southern seashore; Nantes, fifty miles east of the Loire River mouth; and the many small harbors and beaches useful for discharging cargo. If Brittany could be captured, one of the basic requirements for the success of the Allied invasion would be fulfilled: a large port with the capacity to support the forces deemed necessary to defeat the Germans. Without the capture of these seaports, the Allies, particularly the Americans, did not believe they could sustain the buildup of forces needed to advance on Germany. As General Eisenhower would state, "The ideal situation would be to obtain the entire coastal area from Havre to Nantes, both inclusive. With such a broad avenue of entry we could bring to the Continent [France] every single soldier the United States could procure for us."

To gain a broad avenue of entry was a major Allied objective. It had long been planned to turn the VIII Corps westward into Brittany

as soon as the Americans reached the French town of Avranches. In moving toward the French towns Rennes and St. Malo, the VIII Corps was suppose to precede other units of the Third Army, which would then clear the whole of the Brittany Peninsula.

General Bradley thus ordered Patton to drive southward to seize the cities of Rennes and Fougres, then turn westward to secure the towns of St. Malo, Quiberon Bay, the city of Brest, and the remainder of Brittany, in that order. American military support formations were alerted to the job of opening and developing the ports of St. Malo, Quiberon Bay, and Brest as soon as possible after their capture.

Before the invasion of France, the Allies had thought it would be necessary to divert a sizable US force to capture the Breton ports. When German forces started to break apart in confusion and retreat from the advancing American Army, the opportunity of seizing Brittany with much smaller forces became posible. Specifically, General Patton planned to drive southwest from Avranches through Rennes to Quiberon Bay in order to cut the

Robert Russo, a Sherman tank commander who saw action in France, described a nighttime battle encounter in his unit's history: "I was just about dozing off when all hell broke loose. I heard a large explosion, followed by another and still another; I looked through the periscope and saw that three tanks in front of me were burning fiercely. Through my mind ran the thought of my trapped buddies; you can imagine how I felt. From that moment on, everything seemed to be a madhouse. I could see figures running back and forth, silhouetted by the flames of the burning tanks." Pictured is a burned out Sherman tank fitted with a dozer blade. *Patton Museum*

General John Shirley Wood, commander of the 4th Armored Division, was an aggressive commander who always strove to knock the enemy off balance through daring, violent action. He did not, however, expend the lives of his men freely. He weighed every tactical decision on the grounds that the lives of his soldiers were an investment that demanded an appropriate military return. Pictured is a destroyed German Mark IV medium tank.
Patton Museum

Brittany peninsula near its base and prevent the reinforcement or escape of German forces already there.

Next, Patton would clear Brittany by seizing the central plateau of the peninsula. In so doing, he would liberate a vast region of France, open interior lines of communication, and reduce the German defenses to isolated pockets along the coastal regions. With the Germans penned into a few port cities, it was belived that it would be relatively easy to force their surrender. Once the ports were in American hands, the Third Army would be free to turn east, where the decisive battle of the European campaign would obviously be fought. Thus, Patton visualized his primary mission as clearing the peninsula, his secondary mission as securing Quiberon Bay and Brest first and the other ports later, his eventual mission as driving eastward toward Paris and the Seine River.

Patton's method for securing Brittany was to unleash armored columns in the peninsula. The 4th Armored Division was to drive through the city of Rennes to Quiberon. The 6th Armored Division was to go all the way to Brest. A third column, formed by activating a provisional unit called Task Force A under the command of Brig. General Herbert L. Earnest, was to advance to Brest to secure the vital railroad that follows generally the north shore.

If Brest was to prove of value as a port of entry, the double-track railway linking it to the city of Rennes had to be in good condition. Since the railroad crossed several large bridges that could not be quickly or easily replaced or

ABOVE
Next to the 4th Armored Division, the only other armored division to spend as much time under the command of Patton's Third Army in Europe was the famous 6th Armored Division, nicknamed the "Super Sixth," under the very capable command of Major General Robert W. Crow. Patton's chief of staff stated that the "Super Sixth" was one of the most dependable divisions that served in the Third Army during the drive across France and then into Germany. Pictured is the crew of a Sherman watching a female prisoner being guarded by members of the French underground. *Patton Museum*

To help keep track of his far-ranging armored divisions during the Third Army's spectacular dash across France in 1944, Patton reformed the 6th Cavalry Group into an Army Information Service. Normal signal communications and command channels were bypassed. Information that was obtained by patrols on the front lines was instantly relayed by radio and teletype to Third Army Headquarters. Pictured is a Dodge command car outfitted with a radio. *Patton Museum*

repaired; Task Force A was to capture the bridges before the Germans could demolish them. That Patton considered this an important mission was clear when he requested General Robert Grow of the 6th Armored Division to also keep an eye out for the bridges along the railroad, particularly the one at Morlaix.

Patton, unlike General Bradley, considered the capture of St. Malo incidental to the entire

Brittany campaign. He did not specifically assign it as an objective to any of his forces. And he apparently influenced Bradley to the extent that Bradley agreed that St. Malo could be bypassed and contained if its capture appeared to require too many forces and too much time.

Unlike Eisenhower and Bradley, who seemed to be more intent in rounding up every German soldier cut off by the Allied invasion of France, Patton always saw his immediate objectives far in advance of any front-line position. His main goal was always to slash forward and exploit not only the mobility and striking power of his armored divisions, but also to take advantage of any German disorganization. To accomplish these goals Patton typically granted his divisional commanders a freedom of action that permitted them to be virtually independent.

To keep up with what his divisional commander would be doing out in the field, Patton needed some way of staying in touch with them. To have this ability, Patton decided to convert one of his reconnaissance units into a fast moving communications unit.

In this newly formed organization, a varying number of ex-reconnaissance platoons (each usually with two officers, twenty-eight men, six armored cars, and six jeeps) were formed into small units that were to report the activities of combat units down through battalion size. These reconnaissance platoons were to funnel information through their headquarter's unit. Which would then coordinate and condense any information into teletype messages and send it directly to the Third Army's advance-command post.

This ad-hoc unit would become known as Patton's Household Cavalry and was required to bypass normal communications channels. On many occasions this meant that Patton would be better informed on what was happing with his

Lieutenant Colonel R. W. Jenna, who saw combat in Europe, stated in a wartime report: "The German Volkswagen in no way comes up to the standards of our 1/4-ton truck [jeep]. The German vehicle has a four-cylinder air-cooled engine, which is low in power and performance, while our liquid-cooled four-cylinder engine gives more than ample power and speed through a power train offering a wide selection of gear ratios." Pictured is a privately owned World War II German Volkswagen in use during the Patton Museum's annual forth of July living history show. *Richard Pemberton*

Lieutenant Colonel Jenna went on his report to state: "The Volkswagen has a very low center of gravity, a feature which is not too important in a military vehicle. To obtain this feature the vehicle is made very low and is unable to travel over extremely rough or rocky terrain where our 1/4-ton truck [jeep] performs at its best." Pictured is a very early version of the jeep taking to the air. *Patton Museum*

divisions in the field then the divisional and Corps officers directing the actual operation.

Since long before the D-day invasion, Allied tactical ground-attack aircraft had concentrated on bridge-busting, a very effective way of slowing German movement. General Patton looked at it in a different way. He wanted the bridges intact so that his own tanks and troops could cross the rivers without delay, without having to ford or build pontoon bridges.

Patton always wanted advances to happen quickly and he did his best to make them happen. Within five days all of Brittany except the French towns and cities of Brest, St. Malo, Lie de Cezembre, and Lorient were in American hands. The very speed of Third Army movement changed the whole character of fighter-bomber cooperation. Before Patton's tank division broke through German lines, the highest priority assignment for American P-47 Thunderbolts, P-51 Mustangs, and P-38 Lightnings had been the isolation of the battlefield from

the south, east, and north of the American invasion bridgehead positions. That assignment was based on the thought that the American military advance into the heartland of France would be slow and tortuous and that it was advantageous to demolish permanent road and river structures such as bridges, embankments, and overpasses to stop the Germans from getting their tanks and soldiers to the battle zone. When General Patton started moving, he turned the interdiction job inside out. The Third Army wanted fighter-bombers to prevent movement from, not to, the battle area. It wanted the German escape roads blocked, but it also wanted lines of communication and the transportation infrastructure ahead of its troops as undamaged as possible.

Before Patton's Third Army was activated, one of the highest priority assignment for US Army Air Force units supporting the First Army's stubborn drive into France was the attacking of German defensive positions that had held out for days and might continue for weeks. American fighter-bomber units could make detailed plans up to twenty-four to forty-eight hours in advance before attacking German defensive positions.

Under Patton's Third Army command, the Army Air Forces' role, missions, and tactics were completely reversed. There were no such things as German "strong points" in Brittany, short of the great island and port fortresses. Over the open country of the peninsula, the Germans rarely paused long enough to make a stand on Hill X or Ridge Y. It became impossible for the US Army Air Forces to plan tactical air cooperation missions a day in advance when Third Army tanks were rolled ahead almost twenty miles a day. It soon became clear that in cooperating with General Patton, the US Army Air Forces would have to find its targets in the field and then plan its missions as it flew them.

Like their boss Patton, General John Wood of the 4th Armored Division and General Robert Grow of the 6th Armored Division were both true believers in the power of fast-moving armored columns. This was just the opposite of their corps commander, General Troy Middleton, who was an infantryman from the old school. Middleton reported to Patton. Wood and Grow were convinced they understood better what Patton expected. Their units had been relatively untouched by the bloody combat in the French hedgerows and had not sustained the heavy losses that had been inflicted on other units already engaged in combat with the Germans. Having thrust victoriously to Avranches in the last days of July, they believed they had accomplished what other units had not been able to do. Having led the US forces from the breakthrough into the break out, these two divisional commanders and their units became infected with an enthusiasm and a self-confidence that were perfectly suited to exploitation, but proved to be a headache to those who sought to retain a traditional semblance of control.

The M8 armored car was a lightly armored four-man, six-wheeled, seven-ton vehicle. It was supposed to provide high-speed mobility, defensive firepower, and crew protection for reconnaissance personnel. The armament consisted of a single 37mm cannon with one co-axial .30-caliber machine gun in a manually operated turret. Normally there was also a .50-caliber machine gun on a pedestal mount located on top of the vehicle's turret. *Patton Museum*

Unfortunately, by the time the American M8 armored car reached the field, it was obsolete for the reconnaissance role it was intended for. According to Lieutenant Colonel John A. Beall: "The armor on the M8 is unsatisfactory and gives the crew little or no protection against any-caliber AT [antitank] weapon. Grenades can be easily thrown into the vehicle by enemy infantry. The 37mm gun on the M8 is wholly inadequate as an antitank weapon." This is an overhead shot of an M8 armored car. *Patton Museum*

With Patton's corps units stretched over a vast area of France and moving rapidly, signal communications (radio and wire) broke down almost completely. The expensive signal equipment at the disposal of the corps-level commanders was never designed for a penetration and pursuit of the magnitude the Third Army made during the Brittany operation.

It proved to be impossible to install or maintain wire communications over such distances. During the night of August 3, 1944, the few corps signal lines to forward units that did exist were knocked out by German planes, as were the wires to the army headquarters from which Patton oversaw his corps commanders and their divisions.

Although Patton's communications with both the 4th and 6th armored divisions were sometimes tenuous at times, they were particularly weak in the case of the 6th Armored Division, which had disappeared in a cloud of dust on the roads to Brest. Since Signal Corps per-

A cousin of the M8 armored car was the M20, based on the same basic chassis as the M8. The big difference in the M20 was the lack of a turret. Instead, a large open compartment took up the center of the vehicle. In this configuration, the vehicle was designated as an armored utility car and was considered suitable for a number of different roles. Armament on the M20 consisted of a single ring-mounted .50-caliber machine gun. *Patton Museum*

Some of the roles undertaken by the US Army's M20s during World War II included some of the same scouting duties as performed by the M8 armored car. Like the M8, the M20 suffered from the same drawbacks in combat. Its open top meant that its crew was exposed to artillery and mortar fire, since no overhead protection was provided. Even worse, to use the vehicle's onboard .50-caliber machine gun, the gunner had to expose his entire upper body to enemy fire. Pictured is an M20 being used in the scouting role. *Patton Museum*

sonnel were unable to lay telephone cables fast enough and far enough, the division depended to a large extent on the high-powered SCR-399 long-distance radio, which proved inadequate for the task. As many as eight different transmitters working on the assigned corps frequency were often heard at the same time. With the corps radio communications net so jammed and signals so faint because of distance, the armored divisions had to wait for radio time. Often a code group had to be repeated six to ten times to ensure accurate reception.

A corps cable teletype team had been attached to the 6th Armored Division in the early part of the D-Day invasion, but it had been unable to keep up with the rapid advance and was replaced in Brittany by a radio teletype team using very high-frequency beam antenna equipment. The new team was instructed to place its equipment on a prominent hill near Avranches France where the corps expected to place a receiving station on August 1, 1944. Be-

cause the Germans were still dug in on the hill and because German planes were attacking US troops and installations in the Avranches area, the corps signal section set up its receiving station near Bréhalj France instead. Without knowing of this change of location, the division radio teletype team beamed in on the wrong place. Had the distance between sender and receiver been shorter, the correct location would have been easily found, but beyond fifty miles, the equipment was unreliable, and contact was not established for several days.

With Patton's radio teletype equipment nonoperational, with high-power radio erratic, and with wire and cable lacking, communications often depended upon messengers who traveled long distances by jeep. Sometimes a round trip between a division and a corps headquarters could take the better part of a day. Messengers were excellent targets for bypassed enemy groups and individual snipers in the far-reaching no man's land between the

THIS PAGE AND NEXT PAGE
Another of Patton's personal command vehicles was this Dodge 3/4-ton command reconnaissance car, shown in these four different views shortly after being modified for Patton by Army depot personnel. Clearly visible in one shot of the vehicle are Patton's must-have large air horns. Also visible in the same picture is the vehicle-mounted winch and a small armored shield for the vehicle's radiator. *Patton Museum*

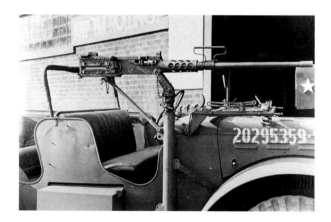

corps and division command posts, and they had to have a lot of patience and luck to get through sometimes.

Because of all these difficulties, the interval between the sending of a message and the receipt of its acknowledgment from the addressee sometimes took up to thirty-six hours. Before the end of the first week in August, the 6th Armored Division was about 150 miles west of Avranches. It was so far away from the corps that General Middleton advised Patton that he had practically no control and little knowledge of his division's operation, and thus denied any responsibility for the division activities. "This headquarters," he wrote Patton, "has made repeated attempts to establish radio contact with the 6th Armored Division without success. A special messenger was dispatched, but his time of arrival cannot be stated. This headquarters will continue efforts to establish radio contact . . ."

As fluid as the situation was to become in Brittany, the immediate preliminary to it was quite the opposite. Getting troops out of Normandy and into Brittany was a difficult problem. In the coastal sector of the original D-Day landing areas there were only two main highways running southward, and debris, dead animals, and wrecked vehicles, as well as mines, and obstructed traffic, while destroyed villages and damaged towns blocked. Army bulldozers had had to clear lanes through rubble

Patton's idea for changing his 6th Cavalry Group into an Army Information Service unit was based on his experience in Sicily, where contact between fast-moving armored formations was very hard to maintain at times. Patton knew that any good army commander had to have current and continuous information on what his front-line units were doing. Pictured here passing through a small French town in 1944 is an M20 armored utility vehicle. *Patton Museum*

in some places—particularly at the French town of Avranches before normal military traffic could pass.

Several bridges over the Seine and the Selune Rivers, and the road approaches to these crossing sites, plus the dams nearby, were of extreme importance. During the first few days of August the Luftwaffe appeared in relative strength over this area in a belated effort to block by bombardment the American entrance into Brittany. American anti-aircraft units, a matter of small importance during July, became a vital part of the breakout and exploitation of Patton's Third Army into France. Gun crews, enthusiastic that they had an opportunity at last to participate in action against the enemy, shot down more than a score of planes around Avranches during the first week of August.

Though combat operations in Brittany later diminished in importance, the prospect of success at the beginning of August led to high expectations among American and other Allied

Patton's Army Information Service unit (also nicknamed "Patton's Household Cavalry"), using jeeps and M8 and M20 armored cars, did their job so well during their time as Patton's eyes and ears that at no time was Patton or his staff ignorant of the disposition or situation confronting any of his major units. Pictured is the crew of an M8 armored car being cheered by a group of French priests. *Patton Museum*

The M10 Tank Destroyer, which had been introduced into the US Army inventory during the 1943 Tunisian campaign, was still in use when Patton's Third Army started its advance across France in August 1944. Unfortunately, while the M10s in North Africa had attained a semblance of qualitative parity with the Germans in antitank firepower, by late 1944 it was completely unequal to the task of neutralizing German tanks. Pictured on the move, the crew of this M10 have added a layer of sandbags to the front hull of their vehicle for added protection. *Patton Museum*

military leaders. The fight for the Normandy beachhead area had been slow and painful; Brittany appeared to be fast and exhilarating. For Patton, one major fact stood out to him. The German military had very little strength to oppose his planned advances into the heart of France.

The March Across France

Confusion of purpose and method on the American side, which was to mar the breakout, stemmed from the abruptness of the change from static to mobile warfare and from the strong contrasting personalities of the military leaders involved. With speed being of the essence, the Americans broke out of the original D-Day landing areas into the relative freedom of a war of movement in Brittany, a difference that seemed to be symbolized by the man of the hour, General Patton.

Patton typified the tenets of daring and dash. If he seemed to be reckless and impetuous to his bosses, he could also be bold and

Even during its use in North Africa many American military officers considered the entire concept of tank destroyers, including the M10, to be a waste of time and money. Major General John P. Lucas, a special observer in Tunisia, reported that "the Tank Destroyer has, in my opinion, failed to prove its usefulness . . . . I believe that the doctrine of an offensive weapon 'to slug it out' with the tank is unsound." Pictured on display at the Patton Museum is an example of an M10. *Michael Green*

imaginative, favoring a "good plan violently executed now" rather than "a perfect plan next week." Like Napoleon, he believed that war was a very simple thing. Its determining charateristics "were self-confidence, speed, and audacity." During August 1944, Patton was to find a situation perfectly suited to implement his belief on how modern war should be fought.

Because of Patton's personality, the headquarters of the Third Army functioned somewhat differently than Omar Bradley's First Army headquarters. From the official United States Army history of World War II comes this extract: "The difference was evident only by comparison. The First Army tended to be more methodical and meticulous in staff work, and required more reports from subordinate units. More planning was committed to paper in the First Army, wheras informal briefings and conversations frequently suf-

ficed in the Third. Yet in both armies the work of the staff members was neither underrated nor unappreciated. Long hours of patient staff work often preceded a daring decision or brought a brilliant idea to maturity and reality. The many anonymous staff officers who toiled in relative obscurity, not only on the army level but on all echelons of command, made it possible for the military leaders of World War II to direct the complex operations with such apparent ease."

By mid-August 1944, Patton's 4th Armored Division was tasked with the mission of guarding the extreme southern flank of the Allied forces as they moved eastward across France. By August 21, the division was moving in a long column through the outskirts of the French city Orleans to the city of Sens. Little German opposition was encountered, and the division reached Sens before dark, arriving just in time to capture a full train of Ger-

LEFT
Pictured looking down into the open-topped turret of an M10 Tank Destroyer is the breech end of the modified 3in naval gun mounted in the vehicle. This gun proved unable to penetrate the thicker armor found on German tanks in the 1944–45 period. In a wartime report, Technician Grade Five Earnest B. Foster describes a combat engagement involving M10s: "I saw three dug-in Tank Destroyers with 3in Naval guns open fire on two Mark Vs at a range of 800 yards, resulting in two ricochets on the German tanks and two tank destroyers knocked out, the third one withdrawing." *Patton Museum*

man gasoline before pulling into the town. This prize lifted some of the burden from the lengthening supply line.

The 4th Armored Division continued its drive, crossing the Yonne, Seine, and Marne Rivers and reaching the French city of Ligny.

During the war, M10 crews spoke highly of their vehicle despite its firepower disadvantages. According to a wartime report: "Crews especially admired the M10 for its versatility and for the reliability of its twin diesel engines, although they felt that it would be improved by the addition of a power-traverse turret, a machine gun mounted for employment against ground targets, and a turret cover for protection against small-arms fire." Shown in this overhead shot is the entire crew of an M10 in the bottom of the vehicle's turret. *Patton Museum*

Never losing sight of his armored division being only part of a combined-arms team, Patton depended heavily on air-ground cooperation during his drive across France. General O. P. Weyland, commander of the XIX Tactical Air Command, supported Patton by using his ground-attack aircraft to cut off enemy lines of retreat, to destroy armored vehicles and infantry in flight retreat, and to eliminate any pockets of resistance or delaying actions by German units. Pictured is a German half-track destroyed by American fighter bombers. *Patton Museum*

Since breaking the German lines in Normandy, the 4th Armored Division had advanced through Axis territory more than 700 miles and had continually spearheaded the front corps of Patton's Third Army. The majority of the division's combat vehicles travelled in excess of 1,500 miles, while many supply vehicles had covered more than 3,000 miles.

As August 1944 ended, 70,000 Germans had passed through Third Army prisoner-of-war compounds, and Patton's forces were fighting at the approaches to the Siegfried Line. Except for some miscellaneous cleaning up and some extremely hard frontier fighting, the Battle of France was over, and the Battle of Germany had begun.

Operations of Patton's Third Army as they developed during September 1944 underwent an abrupt change as the history-making pace of the Army's August 1944 advance was slowed, making necessary a type of warfare considerably different from that employed during the first thirty-one days of action in France. At the beginning of the month, it was apparent that, whatever the cause, an acute shortage of gasoline was seriously impairing the Army's mobility. Subsequently came other supply shortages, plus an enemy build-up and steadily worsening weather conditions. By the end of September, the Third Army had gone from an offensive to a defensive status.

General Weyland used his planes in two types of operations in support of Patton's Third Army drive across France. The first was called armed reconnaissance. In these operations, American fighter-bombers armed with bombs and bullets would roam ahead of Patton's advancing armored columns to attack targets of opportunity. These missions paid great dividends in locating and breaking up potential German counterattacks before they could be launched. Pictured after the battle are some American airmen visiting examples of their handiwork. In this case a destroyed Panther tank. *Patton Museum*

Patton's 4th Armored Division had to end its active pursuit of the Germans across France when a fuel shortage developed on September 2, 1944. They were forced to end all large-scale activity until September 10, when a unit from the division found 100,000 gallons of German gasoline in an abandoned French railroad yard. With this new supply of fuel, the division was ordered on September 11 to secure a bridgehead on the Moselle River south of the French city of Nancy.

The establishment of the bridgehead on the Moselle occupied the division until October 12. During this period, the 4th Armored Division took part in one of the largest armored battles on the western front. Engaging two Panzer brigades and two full Panzer divisions, the 4th Armored destroyed 236 German tanks in the general area from which the Germans launched the assault. A Waffen SS colonel captured by the division on September 15, when interrogated, paid tribute to the division by remarking: "I would be pleased to know the commander of this particular division and I am sure it must be part of General Patton's Third Army. General Patton is for the American Army what General Rommel stands for in the German Army, but to know the commander of this armored division would explain to me how this army managed to achieve such a spurt of advance, which in many instances caught us completely unprepared."

The second type of mission flown by General Weyland's pilots was aimed at direct support of Third Army armored columns. Between ten to fourteen tanks in every armored division were equipped with the same VHF radio sets carried by American fighter aircraft. Four- to eight-ship flights would hover over the lead elements of an armored column, ready to attack on request, to warn the tanks of hidden opposition, and to eliminate enemy delaying actions. Pictured is a German StuG III assault gun and crew that got in the way of American ground-attack aircraft. *Patton Museum*

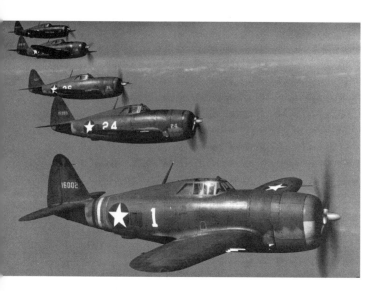

The campaign during the month of September can be considered from four phases: First, the slowing of the Third Army's offensive, whereupon a fleeing and badly beaten enemy turned around at the German border and occupied the

In grateful appreciation of the efforts of the Army Air Forces on Third Army's behalf, Patton wrote a letter of commendation to Army Air Forces commander General Weyland in mid-August 1944: "Due to the tireless efforts of your flyers, large numbers of hostile vehicles and troop concentrations ahead of our advancing columns have been harassed or obliterated. The information passed directly to the head of the columns from the air has saved times and lives." Pictured is a flight of P-47 Thunderbolts, the type of aircraft that took such a heavy toll of German men and equipment while supporting Patton's Third Army. *Patton Museum*

Moselle River line; second, the battle in which the enemy fought desperately to prevent crossings of the Moselle and Meurthe Rivers and launched counterattacks against the north and south flanks of the Third Army; third, developments along the flanks; and fourth, the end of the Army's activities in the Brittany Peninsula.

The Third Army's major activity during October 1944 was concentrated on building up its supplies, assembling and regrouping troops, and laying plans (including carrying on of limited-objective operations) all in preparation for a new major offensive designed to drive the Germans back across the Rhine River. Re-examination of the entire supply system was made to conserve weapons and ammunition, and to obtain all possible benefits from the supplies on hand. Also accomplished was equipping troops with adequate wet- and cold-weather clothing and bringing armored and other vehicles to top condition. Planning activities for the new offensive included the execution of certain limited objective operations to secure a favorable line of departure to keep the Germans from becoming too aggressive, and to give specialized combat experience to various units. The XII

Corps carried on such offensives successfully during the month. The XX Corps operations against various forts protecting the French city of Metz provided a basis for training troops in assaults on fixed fortifications and served to determine the tactical plan for future operations against the fortress city of Metz itself.

Major contact with the Germans resulted with the XII Corps' drive to enlarge and improve its bridgehead east of the Moselle and Meurthe Rivers and the Third Army's effort to wipe out the enemy's bridgehead west of Metz. Aggressive and determined German opposition met both of these offensives.

By October 1, 1944, the German High Command realized that the current threat to the stability of their front lines did not exist in Patton's Third Army zone. The German counterattacks against Patton's XII Corps died down rapidly as the Germans reshuffled their forces

The 6th Armored Division was first committed to action in France on July 29, 1944. Both the 4th and 6th armored divisions were configured in 1944 as relatively light but powerful formations with roughly 11,000 officers and men each. Both divisions had a typical inventory of 263 light and medium tanks and about 54 artillery pieces. In both divisions, the major fighting elements were in three tank battalions, three battalions of armored infantry, and three battalions of self-propelled field artillery. Pictured is an M7 self-propelled chassis mounting a 105mm howitzer. *Patton Museum*

Each tank battalion within the 4th and 6th Armored Divisions consisted of one company equipped with M5 or M5A1 light tanks and three companies equipped with various models of the M4 Sherman medium tank. Most of the Sherman tanks landed after D-Day were still armed with the same obsolete low-velocity 75mm gun they had when they rolled off their landing craft during the November 1942 invasion of French North Africa. Pictured coming off an LST are early-model Shermans armed with the low-velocity 75mm gun. *Patton Museum*

RIGHT TOP
According to US Army tanker Sergeant Sulpher Shull and his crew: "It seems that the general opinion back home in the States is that American tanks are second to none. But anyone who has had any actual experience could tell you without a doubt, that our tanks don't compare with those of the Germans in many ways." Pictured is a Sherman tank that took a high-velocity round in its turret and burned out. *Patton Museum*

RIGHT BOTTOM
Corporal Arthur A. Deludea, a tank gunner in Europe, stated in a wartime report: "I have seen enemy heavy tanks hit as high as fifteen times without phasing them. I am not going to try to compare the German tank with our Sherman-mounted 75mm gun. They are just all around better weapons of war. They are heavier, have better guns, better sights, flotation, and more armor. I know that our fighting men can out-fight the Germans, and we in the armored force feel that we need tanks at least equal to theirs." Pictured on display at the Patton Museum is this German Panther tank. This vehicle is missing its tracks. *Michael Green*

and sent their better-trained and more mobile elements to meet the growing major threats in Holland, at Aachen and in the Seventh Army zone. By the end of October, the German strength opposing the Third Army was estimated at only five divisions.

German air activity was also in very limited scale during October 1944, as compared to August and September. Only when a serious threat to vital areas developed was any large-scale effort made by the Luftwaffe. Anti-aircraft claims by the Third Army for the month were only twenty-seven planes destroyed or probably destroyed, bringing the total to 461 since beginning of operations.

It wouldn't be until November 1944 that Patton's Third Army would go back on the offensive after having been on the defense, because of an acute supply situation, since September 25, 1944.

The Battle of Germany

On November 8, 1944, the Third Army opened the battle of Germany, thereby upsetting the German's hopes for a winter breathing spell. Patton's XII Corps delivered the first of a two-blow attack, preceded by a devastating artillery preparation that disrupted German communications and curtailed the employment of their artillery.

The Seine and Moselle Rivers, which happened to be at flood stage as the result of the unusually heavy autumn rains, imposed an unforeseen obstacle to Third Army troops and their advance. On November 9, 1944, when the XX Corps delivered the second punch, the rivers were at record high levels. Bridgeheads that had been won by the 5th, 80th, 90th, and 95th infantry divisions were maintained only by the utmost effort. At the beginning of the month, the Germans committed on the Third Army front an estimated 42,500 troops, the equivalent of five divisions. These included major elements of six infantry divisions, one panzer-grenadier division, and five infantry and machine-gun battalions. The 11th Panzer Division, while out of contact, was believed to be in immediate reserve on the Third Army front. Patton's attack on November 8, 1944, provoked an immediate reaction. Drawing upon tactical reserves and shifting elements of divisions on adjacent fronts, the Germans increased their total commitments to an estimated eight divisions, consisting of 63,500 troops and 285 tanks by the end of the first week of the offensive. In addition to these reinforcements, the Germans bolstered their battered forces by the hasty commitment of units from defensive positions in the Siegfried Line.

Bad weather throughout the entire month greatly hampered the Third Army's opera-

In a wartime report dated from late 1944, US Army Lieutenant Colonel Wilson M. Hawkins stated: "We have been outgunned since Tunisia, when the German brought out their Mark IV Special with the long-barreled 75mm gun. The higher muzzle velocity of the German gun increases their accuracy, as range estimation is of less importance with such a flat trajectory." Pictured is a late-war Mark IV with its long-barreled 75mm gun. *Patton Museum*

Captain W. Johnson compared M4 Shermans with enemy tanks in a wartime report: "In general, it is my opinion that our Sherman tanks rank clumsily with the German Mark III and Mark IV tanks, and their Mark V and Mark VI tanks are in a class by themselves, having a better silhouette, better armor, better flotation and maneuverability, far better guns with much better sight reticules, and superior ammunition." Pictured is a Mark V (Panther) tank in France. *Frank Schulz*

tions, limiting the use of air support and confining armor and tank destroyers largely to roads, and the Germans took every advantage of the defensive opportunities afforded by the weather. German troops were moved and reinforcements committed with comparative immunity from American air attack. The German military forces used demolitions and mines in conjuction with frequent roadblocks and blown bridges covered by antitank fire to harass the Third Army's armored spearheads. Numerous German counterattacks, principally of company strength supported by a few tanks, were launched at critical points in an effort to contain Patton's eastward thrusts.

The Germans fought delaying action from one critical terrain feature to the next. Practically every village was turned into a defensive strong point and maximum use was made of the limited amount of artillery the Germans still had.

Despite reinforcements committed by the Germans, the estimated strength opposing the Third Army by the end of the second week of the offensive dropped to the equivalent of seven divisions (56,000 troops) and 165 tanks, as a result of heavy losses sustained in their counterattacks. During the last week of the month, the German's strength further decreased to the equivalent of five divisions (39,000 troops) and 140 tanks, again due to the heavy losses, among them 25,592 prisoners of war.

November 1944 saw a further decrease in German air activity over the Third Army area, with 78 raids by 136 aircraft, of which 16 attacked ground targets. Of these, anti-aircraft units claimed 16 destroyed and 11 probably destroyed.

December operations of the Third Army were divided into two phases. As the month began, the Army was advancing toward the Siegfried Line in continuation of the operation that had opened on November 8, 1944, succeeding during the early part of the month in capturing the remaining forts at Metz, a feat unprecedented in modern history.

During the first fifteen days of December, the Germans continued to fight a delaying action all along the Third Army's front. The XII and XX Corps continued their assault of the German defensive positions, which had started on November 8, 1944. Unfortunately, poor weather conditions restricted US Army movement to roads and prevented effective air support. Because of this, the Germans succeeded in pre-

Colonel S. R. Hind, who saw heavy combat in Europe, stated in a wartime report: "In my opinion, the reason our armor has engaged the German tanks as successfully as it has is not due by any means to a superior tank but to our superior numbers of tanks on the battlefield and the willingness of our tankers to take their losses while maneuvering to a position from which a penetrating shot can be put through a weak spot of the enemy tank." Shown is a Panther tank that took multiple hits in its weaker flank armor. *Patton Museum*

venting a major breakthrough by Patton's forces. However, under continuous pressure from the Third Army, the Germans slowly withdrew into their Siegfried Line defenses behind the Saar River. Despite stubborn resistance and continuous counterattacks, the Germans were unable to prevent the establishment of three Third Army bridgeheads across the Saar, in the Saarlautern Dillingen area, between December 3 and 6, 1944. Bitter fighting continued in the bridgehead areas until the relaxation of the Third Army's attacks in order to deal with the Germans Ardennes offensive.

During their withdrawal into the Siegfried Line, the Germans sustained heavy losses. As a result, their strength on the Third Army front was reduced from the equivalent of five divisions of combat effectiveness on December 1, 1944, to the equivalent of four divisions by December 15, 1944.

An all-out attack was planned for December 19, 1944, at which time XII and XX Corps, plus III Corps (which had become operational and held positions in the central part of the Army zone) were to speed up their attack with the mission of smashing through the remaining Siegfried Line fortifications and driving for the Rhine River. It was necessary, however, to call off this attack because of the German attack in the Ardennes.

Corporal Francis E. Vierling, a tank commander in Europe, expressed his total frustration in a wartime report with the poor combat performance of the 75mm gun mounted in the Sherman tank: "To see twenty-five or even many more of our rounds fired and ricochet off the enemy attackers. To be finally hit, once, and we climb from and leave a burning, blacked and now a useless pile of scrap iron. It would have yet been a tank had it mounted a gun." Pictured is a Sherman that took a direct hit through its frontal armor and then burned. *Patton Museum*

Sergeant Robbins M. Rains, a Sherman tank commander, and his driver stated in a wartime report: "Since landing in France with this division, we've seen countless numbers of American tanks knocked out and burned with a resultant high loss of American lives, due, we believe, to our inferior tanks." Pictured is a Sherman tank, which—due to internal explosions—has lost not only its turret, but, almost the entire hull has been blown apart. *Fred Ropkey*

RIGHT
Sergeant Harold S. Rathburna, Sherman tank commander in Europe, compared his tank to German tanks in a wartime report: "In past engagements with the enemy, we have placed tank against tank very often. In one tank battle, our M4 was hit in the front by an AP [armor piercing] shell from a Mark VI. It went in the front and came out the rear. I have also seen our 75mm AP shells bounce off the front of the Mark V and Mark VI tanks." Pictured is a Tiger I's long-barreled 88mm gun. *Patton Museum*

Corporal Thomas G. Mclane stated in a wartime report: "I joined this organization in France and have been with it ever since. I have seen quite a few of our M4 tanks pierced and exploded by deflect [hits] of the German 75 projectiles. In my estimation the German Mark V tank is superior to our medium tank, M4, in both armor and armament. Our successes in Europe are a result of superiority in numbers and superiority in good cold guts, not a result of superior tanks." Pictured in France in 1944 is this excellent shot of the front and rear of two camouflaged Panther tanks. *Frank Schulz*

RIGHT
Only occasionally, under certain tactical situations, was the Sherman low-velocity 75mm gun able to destroy German tanks like the Panther. From the unit history of the 5th Armored Division comes this extract: "That night an unusual scrap occurred at one of the road blocks which had been hastily set up. A Mark V tank, rumbling through the darkness, rammed head on into a tank from C Company, 81st Tank Battalion. The Sherman's 75mm gun immediately belched out a round of armor-piercing ammunition which struck the gun mantle on the Mark V and was deflected down through the hull, killing the German crew members." Pictured is a destroyed Panther tank being examined by curious American soldiers. *Patton Museum.*

In a wartime report out of Germany, Sherman tank commander Frederick H. Wilson went on record saying: "I have been taught that our tanks have much more maneuverability than the German tanks. It has been proven to me just a few days ago that it isn't so. The German Mark V, which is much heavier than our M4, beats ours around a large-sized field; it makes sharp swerves or reverses of direction in a shorter space than ours can possibly do. German tanks have much wider tracks and do not become bogged down as easily as ours do in muddy terrain." Pictured is a Panther in France 1944, heading off-road. *Frank Schulz*

RIGHT
Sometimes bad weather could actually help the Sherman tanks in battle against the better-protected German tanks. From the unit history of the 4th Armored Division comes this description of what thick ground fog could do to even the odds: "A section of M4 tanks were in an outpost position south of Lezey when the first Panther suddenly loomed out of the fog, hardly 75 yards from the two American tanks. The Panther and two of its fellows were destroyed in a matter of seconds." Pictured is a Panther that had its thick frontal armor penetrated. *Patton Museum*

Despite the fact that most American tankers and their commanding officers considered the M5 light tank completely obsolete as far back as 1942, the M5 light tank (and a slightly improved model known as the M5A1) were still in service in 1944. They would remain in service all the way to the end of the war in Europe. Its The M5's 37mm main gun was useless against German tanks and self-propelled guns. Shown in a posed wartime picture is an M5A1 light tank somewhere in Europe. *Patton Museum*

Bolaslaw Kubacki, a US Army corporal in charge of an M5A1 light tank in Europe, stated in a wartime report: "On July 30, 1944, in the vicinity of Villebadon, France, my M5A1 light tank engaged a Mark IV German tank. The German tank fired at our tank and missed. We immediately returned the fire, hit the enemy tank, but the shell did not penetrate through the enemy armor." Pictured is the crew of an M5A1 light tank firing on enemy positions. *Patton Museum*

From a wartime report, Lieutenant Colonel Wilson M. Hawkins stated: "The light tank is being used for working with the infantry. We subject it to direct fire just as little as we can, for it is realized that the armor will not turn either the German antitank fire or the 37mm gun." Pictured is an M5A1 light tank guarding the flank of the half-track-mounted infantry in the background. *Patton Museum*

LEFT TOP
Corporal Guy D. Knight, a crewman on an
M5A1 light tank, described a brief combat
encounter during World War II: "Meanwhile,
our tank, commanded by Staff Sergeant Wise,
was pulled out of our camouflage onto the
road where we could lay down a covering fire.
We starting firing at a well concealed self-
propelled gun that was covered by a haystack.
Our aim was true but our shells (37mm)
weren't powerful enough to penetrate. An HE
[high explosive] shell hit our tank on the gun
shield, killing our tank commander and
shaking the rest of us pretty badly." Pictured
on display at the British Tank Museum is this
late-war German turretless self-propelled gun.
Paul Handel

LEFT BOTTOM
First Lieutenant Peter Kostow described the use of
his M5A1 light tank in the infantry support role in
a wartime report: "I fired a 37mm cannister
ammunition at eight Germans at a range of
approximately fifty yards. The noise and blast
scared them and they surrendered. Not one of the
eight German was wounded." Shown is a
beautifully restored M5A1 light tank owned by a
private collector in California. *Michael Green*

BELOW
One of the few positive features of the
American M5 and M5A1 light tanks was their
great mechanical reliability. According to
Lieutenant Colonel R. W. Jenna, who stated in a
wartime report: "The twin Cadillac V-8 engines
and Hydromatic Drive Transmission in our light
tanks make it an engineering masterpiece to be
surpassed by none, either now or in the near
future. By actual German admissions they have
lost as many tanks by mechanical failures as
they have by enemy action." Pictured on display
at the Patton Museum's annual living history
display is an M5A1 light tank. *Richard Byrd*

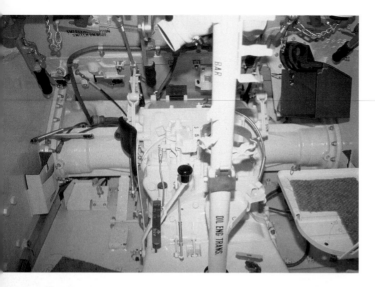

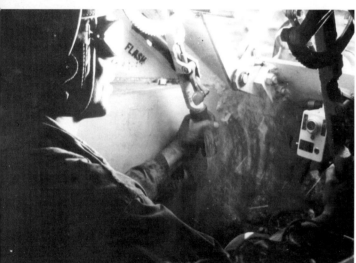

As used in the M5 and M5A1 light tanks, the Hydra-Matic Drive arrangement included two transmissions—one for each engine—and a transfer unit, which combined the power output of the two engines and supplied a two-speed gearing. The four-speed transmissions, in combination with the two-speed transfer unit, provided six forward speeds. These units had automatic shifting features that kept the engines operating in the speed range in which maximum power is developed. Shown in this interior shot of an M5A1 light tank is the front hull. The driver sat on the left-hand side and the assistant driver on the right. *Michael Green*

LEFT BOTTOM
The big advantage of having the automatic shifting features of the Hydra-Matic Drive in the M5 and M5A1 light tanks was to simplify the tank driver's job by eliminating the heavy physical effort of shifting gears. Most all aging tank veterans of World War II can still remember just how hard and tiring it was to shift and drive the Sherman. Pictured is the driver's position in an M5A1 light tank. *Patton Museum*

RIGHT
Mines always played a very important part in German defensive tactics. It was estimated that 16 percent of all American tank losses in Europe were due to mines. The main belt of a large German antitank minefield normally consisted of antitank mines with a sprinkling of antipersonnel mines in the forward edge of the field. Pictured is a Sherman tank that ran over a mine. The open hatches indicate the crew survived the explosion. *Patton Museum*

ABOVE
In general, German World War II mine tactics employed the same basic principles used by the US Army. Maximum use was made of surprise. Natural and artificial barriers were used to force approaching vehicles to cross the minefield. Minefields would be used in conjunction with antitank and supporting-weapon fire. The Germans would often install mines in spurs running at right angles to the forward edge of the minefield to damage vehicles moving along the field in search of lanes. Pictured is an M4 Sherman that had both its tracks damaged by a mine blast. *Patton Museum*

RIGHT TOP
German soldiers often planted mines to catch vehicles off-the-road: narrow places where a passing vehicle might not completely stay on the road and at entrances to defiles where a vehicle might wait for vehicles moving in the opposite direction to pass. Other places frequently mined by the Germans were turn-outs, sharp bends (which fast-moving traffic might overshoot), the unsurfaced islands sometimes found at crossroads, berms, and well-worn wheel ruts. These American soldiers are kidding around with a jeep that had the misfortune of striking a mine. *Patton Museum*

RIGHT BOTTOM
Employing every way possible to hide their mines and minefields, the Germans had some nasty tricks up their sleeves. One of them involved burying mines as much as two feet below the surface so that they would explode only after the passage of a number of vehicles had compacted the earth above the mine sufficiently to actuate the fuse. Pictured is an M4 Sherman that ran into a minefield. *Patton Museum*

RIGHT TOP
The M18 had been designed in 1942 for the US Army as a state-of-the-art tank destroyer. It weighed less than twenty tons and could reach speeds of up to 60mph on a level surface. It was armed with a high-velocity 76mm gun and could run circles around any German tank. The sad part was that the M18 (nicknamed the Hellcat) didn't start coming off the production line until mid-1943. Having even less armor protection than the M10 Tank Destroyer, the speedy M18 couldn't outrun German antitank rounds. The M18 pictured took four rounds through its front hull. *Patton Museum*

RIGHT BOTTOM
Like all armored vehicle designs, the M18 Tank Destroyer was a combination of both good and bad features. Many tank destroyer crewmen spoke very highly of the M18. One military observer in Europe noted that while the First Army refused M18s and stuck with the slightly heavier-armored M10, Patton's Third Army highly valued the M18's speed and extraordinary mobility, which allowed it to accompany cavalry units on scouting missions. Shown is a side view of an M18 Hellcat. *Patton Museum*

LEFT
The German Army had such strict rules about the laying and recording of their minefields that American soldiers could sometimes forecast the location of every mine in a section once the first few were located. German minefields tended to be about 80 x 105ft in size. Normally there would be one mine for each yard of minefield front. Pictured is a soldier unpacking American mines from their packing crate. In the background is an M18 Tank Destroyer. *Patton Museum*

Although American tankers hoped the new 76mm gun would be able to penetrate the frontal armor on German late-war tanks, they were sadly disappointed. Delbert C. Grimmett, who drove a Sherman tank, stated in a wartime report: "I saw an American 76mm on an M4 shoot a German Mark V at a range of 100 feet in the gun shield and not penetrate over 2in. In all cases a 75mm or 76mm gun will not produce results necessary to handle German tanks except from rear or right-angle shots at side armor." Pictured on display in Europe is this early-production, cast-hull M4A1 Sherman armed with a 76mm gun. *Andreas Kirchhoff*

In a vain attempt to improve the firepower of the M4 Sherman tank, the US Army started to mount a 76mm gun in some of them. It was hoped that this larger gun would allow American tankers to take on the German Panther tank. It wasn't to be so. Like the original 75mm gun in the Sherman, the newer 76mm gun proved unequal to the task. Pictured on display in Europe is this early-production, welded-hull M4A3 Sherman armed with a 76mm gun. *Andreas Kirchhoff*

ABOVE
Other models of the Sherman series were also upgraded with the 76mm gun and the new wide-track suspension system. Pictured side-by-side are two different generations of Sherman tanks. On the right is the original narrow-track early-production model M4 Sherman mounting the shorter barrel 75mm gun. On the left is an upgraded M4A1 Sherman with a different turret mounting a 76mm gun and wider tracks. *Michael Green*

LEFT TOP
In August 1944, Chrysler started to build an enhanced model of the M4A3 Sherman tank. While still armed with the same 76mm gun that had already proved itself inadequate in combat with German late-war tanks, the new vehicle had an improved suspension system that featured tracks wider than the earlier Shermans. In this configuration, the vehicle was designated as the M4A3E8. Some tankers would nickname this version of the Sherman as the "Easy Eight." *Patton Museum*

LEFT BOTTOM
What did American tankers think of this new upgraded Sherman with its wider tracks? Major Phillip C. Calhoun stated in a wartime report: "The M4A3E8, with its new type of suspension, is a great improvement in the flotation of our tank." First Lieutenant Coulter M. Montgomery stated in the same report: "We want wider tracks. This new E-8 suspension is a lot better as far as flotation is concerned than our old suspension system, but the German tanks still have better maneuverability in the field." The M4A3E8 Sherman tank pictured is now part of the Pattons Museum's collection of vehicles. *Patton Museum*

In early November 1944, Patton gave a speech to the commanders of the 4th Armored Division in which he stated: "The accomplishments of this division have never been equaled. And by that statement I do not mean in this war, I mean in the entire history of warfare. There has never been such a superb fighting organization as the 4th Armored Division." *Patton Museum*

CHAPTER FIVE

THE BATTLE OF THE BULGE

On the morning of December 16, 1944, the German military launched their Ardennes offensive on a sixty-mile front with five armored divisions and thirteen infantry divisions against the American XII Army Corps (First Army) and the southern portion of the V Corps (First Army). Within this first wave, the Germans had 200,000 men and 500 tanks supported by the fire of almost 2,000 artillery pieces. The opposing American forces whom the Germans would throw themselves at consisted of roughly 83,000 men divided into four divisions. The Americans had 242 medium tanks, 182 tank destroyers, and 394 artillery pieces.

To support the ground assault, the Luftwaffe managed to scrape together almost 1,500 aircraft which came out in force in both day and night operations. From captured documents and prisoner-of-war statements, the top Allied military commanders quickly concluded that the objective of the German attack was the capture of the Belgium cities of Liege and Antwerp and the splitting of the main American and British forces.

The German attack consisted of two prongs: One in the north through Malmedy toward Liege was made by the Sixth SS Panzer Army; the second to the south was made by the Fifth Panzer Army and was aimed at Bastogne and bridgeheads across the Meuse River in Belgium with a thrust to siege the city of Luxembourg.

The only American tank destroyer that was developed during World War II that stood a slight chance at penetrating the frontal armor on the late-war German tanks and self-propelled antitank guns was the M36. The M36 was basically a modified M10 that was fitted with a high-velocity 90mm anti-aircraft gun. The first M36 tank destroyers didn't reach Europe until September 1944. Pictured is a nice frontal shot of an M36. Like the M10, it had no overhead armor protection for the crew. *Patton Museum*

To the top Allied military leaders, it appeared that the northern attack involving initially two panzers, one under-strength paratrooper division, and five infantry divisions was intended as the major effort. Both German advances initially met with success, the northern spearhead driving ahead despite heavy losses at Stavelot, St. Vith, and Malmedy, and the southern spearhead bypassing Bastogne and penetrating into the St. Hubert-Smuid-Tellin-Rocheford area of Belgium.

On December 18, 1944, Patton and his Third Army were directed by higher headquarters to take over all forces south of the German salient, consisting of elements of VIII Corps, and to drive north into the south flank of that salient with the immediate mission being the relief of Bastogne and the use of its road net as a stepping stone for an upcoming drive by the Third Army to relieve St. Vith. This would, in turn, be part of an even larger Allied offensive to kick the Germans out of Belgium all together.

The offensive movement needed to turn the Third Army's striking power to the north was a gigantic and complicated operation involving a switch of the majority of the Third Army's divisions and their supporting troops. Some of the most rapid troop movements in the history of warfare were required across

very difficult terrain in the middle of a freezing European winter. To make matters even more difficult, all these movements had to be combined with a high degree of precise timing and coordination. Not only did the tactical units have to be faced at right angles to the German positions, but the entire supply organization had to follow in support.

By December 17, 1944, the 10th Armored Division which was in Luxembourg, was directed to leave XX Corps for VIII Corps (First Army). In the early morning hours of December 19, the 4th Armored Division, located at Epping-Urbach, eleven miles east of Sarreguemines, moved northward with a task force in the lead. It was followed closely by the 80th Infantry Division, located at Bining, and the 26th Infantry Division, then in training at Metz.

On December 20, 1944, the 5th Infantry Division, located in the Saarlautern bridgehead,

Despite the fitting of the powerful 90mm gun, the only chance the M36 had to destroy late-war German tanks was at very close ranges. In a wartime report, it was the conclusion of the officers and men of the 702nd Tank Destroyer Battalion that "the M36 90mm gun with present ammunition will not penetrate the front slope of a Mark V at greater than 800 yards range as shown by the repeated ricochets in the Puffendorf-Ederen battle." This Mark V is on display at the British Tank Museum. *British Tank Museum*

LEFT
According to Lieutenant Colonel John A. Beall in a wartime report: "Upon interviewing all of my commanders and from my own personal experience, we have all agreed that our frontal armor plate on the M36 is far too light. The Mark V or Mark VI tanks can safely stand off from 1500 to 1600 yards and knock out our M36s at will, achieving penetrations in any part of the hull or turret." Pictured in white wash is an M36 Tank Destroyer. *Patton Museum*

joined the procession. On December 21, sixteen field artillery and six anti-aircraft battalions began the move. On December 22, the 35th Infantry Division, located at Bebelsheim, started for Metz for refitting before being committed. On December 23, a provisional task force of the 6th Armored Division, then located at Lixing, started for the Northern Front.

On December 20, Patton took the time to inspect the assembly positions of the three Army Divisions that would be leading the advance to relieve Bastogne. While Patton and Eisenhower would have preferred to have at least six divisions in the initial assault, Patton did not want to delay his attack any longer than he had to. For Patton, the element of surprise was worth more then any number of additional troops or tanks. Patton gave the order for the American counterattack to begin at 6:00 A.M. on the morning of December 22th.

In a wartime report, the commander of an M36 describes a combat engagement: "The enemy attacked our position with five Mark V tanks. Two of these were destroyed and the others were forced to retreat. Our M36 was lost due to the fact that it had sunk in the soft earth and was unable to maneuver out of an artillery concentration." Pictured is a destroyed Panther tank. *Patton Museum*

Patton's 4th Armored Division entered into the well-known Battle of the Bulge on December 19, 1944, after a 160-mile drive into Belgium which took twenty-one hours to complete. It was during those dark winter days of December 1944 that the Germans, realizing the tide of war had turned, massed an attack through the Ardennes Forest in an attempt to split the Allied advance by driving a wedge northwest to the sea. Pictured are Shermans moving down a snow-covered Belgian road. *Patton Museum*

His plan was to be very simple. His men would advance north in the direction of St. Vith. The 80th Infantry Division, on the right, would maintain contact during its advance with the left wing of the American XII Corps. The 26th Infantry Division would form the center prong of the attack. While the 4th Armored Division would advance on the left towards Bastogne.

Of the three American divisions being used by Patton in his assault on the German southern flank, Patton was most worried about the 4th Armored Division. Considered one of the top American armored divisions of World War II, the 4th had, in the previous months, suffered extremely heavy casualties in men and equipment. It was short of tanks and many of its replacements were green untried troops. Even worse, the division's beloved commander and founder, Gen. John Shirley Wood, had been recently relieved from his post by Patton due to poor health. Many modern historians and veterans of the the 4th Ar-

The German advance into the Ardennes Forest consisted of eleven divisions heavily equipped with as many tanks as the Germans could scrape together at that late stage of the war. By December 21, 1944, the 101st Airborne Division and elements of the 9th and 10th Armored Divisions were encircled in the Belgian town of Bastogne. This photo shows two GIs manning a .30-caliber machine gun in the middle of winter. *Patton Museum*

mored Division believed Wood was relieved by Patton due to a personality conflict. Wood was one of the few senior officers in the Third Army that would stand up to Patton when he felt the lives of his men were being wasted needlessly. To replace General Wood, Patton brought in Maj. Gen. Hugh T. Gaffey, formally the chief of staff of the Third Army.

To make sure that there would be no misunderstandings about his plans for the 4th Armored Division to relieve Bastogne, Patton himself prescribed the tactics to be used by Gaffey and his new command. The attack should begin with tanks, artillery, tank destroyers, and armored engineers in the leading wave. The main body of armored infantry riding in halftracks should be kept back. When heavy German resistance was met, envelop-

ment tactics should be used: no close-in envelopment should be attempted; all envelopments should be started a mile and a half back and be made at right angles. Patton was very aware how dangerous German tanks, like the Panther, could be to his thin-skinned Sherman tanks. He ordered that the new specially armored Sherman tanks known as the Jumbos lead the assault formations. The only problem with the order was that the Third Army only had a few of these tanks in its inventory.

On the morning of December 22, 1944, after days of continual rain, Patton's divisions began their attack north towards Bastogne. On the following day, with the weather changing to clear and cold with flurries of snow, the Army divisions of the XII Corps joined in the attack. The abrupt change in the weather also allowed American planes to go after the German tanks and supply trucks that no longer had the protection of bad weather to hide them from aerial attack.

For Patton, the break in the weather just as his attack began was something he had expected from the Almighty. On December 11, he had ordered the Third Army Chaplain to come up with a prayer that would get him the decent weather he needed from God. The prayer was printed on a small card and handed out to every soldier in the Third Army and read: "Almighty and most merciful Father, we humbly beseech Thee, of Thy great goodness, to restrain these immoderate rains with which we have had to contend. Grant us fair weather for Battle. Graciously hearken to us as soldiers who call upon Thee that armed with thy power, we may advance from victory to victory, and crush the oppression and wickedness of our enemies, and establish Thy justice among men and nations. Amen."

On December 22, Combat Command A and B of the 4th Armored Division attacked abreast of one another towards Bastogne. By the evening of the December 23, Combat Command A was eight miles south of Bastogne. It would be these last few miles to Bastogne that would be the toughest the division would ever have to fight. During the eighteen-day period that the division tried to punch a hole to Bastogne while defending itself from fierce German counterattacks, it would have 214 men killed, 831 wounded, and 56 missing. It would-

By the evening of December 23, 1944, Combat Command A of the 4th Armored Division was only a few miles south of Bastogne. Throughout the day, tankers of the 4th Armored Division could see C-47 transport planes dropping supplies to the surrounded troops in Bastogne. Covered in white wash, this Sherman heads into combat. *Patton Museum*

The last sixteen miles to Bastogne were the toughest the 4th Armored Division ever covered. During the eighteen-day period that the division carved and defended the corridor, it had 214 men killed, 831 wounded, and 56 missing. The hillside villages of Chaumont near Bastogne changed hands three times during the fighting. Shown is a Sherman supporting infantry in a small Belgian town. *Patton Museum*

n't be until December 29 that Bastogne was no longer besieged by the Germans. But the Germans had still not given up. On December 30, the Germans mounted one last counterattack on the 4th Armored Division with a panzer division supported by two infantry divisions and the remnants of a paratrooper division. It would take a week of hard fighting to push the Germans back again. By this point in time the Germans were exhausted. Having taken heavy losses in the campaign and constantly har-

rassed by American aircraft, the Germans would pull their badly mauled divisions back into Germany.

German losses in men and materiel to the Third Army during December 1944, exclusive of Army Air Forces claims, were 67 Mark III and Mark IV medium tanks, 24 Mark VI Tiger tanks, 119 pieces of artillery of 75mm or over, and 178 vehicles of all types. Patton's Third Army lost 17 light tanks, 89 medium tanks, 18 pieces of ar-

The final assault by the 4th Armored Division to break the German stranglehold on Bastogne was launched from the far edge of Assenois, the last village before Bastogne. In the lead was Company C of the 37th Tank Battalion, followed by Company C of the 53rd Armored Infantry. Commander of the 37th Tank Battalion was Lieutenant Colonel Creighton W. Abrams. Driving through a Belgian farm, this white-washed Sherman's rear engine deck is covered with the crew's belongings. *Patton Museum*

RIGHT
To support the final assault by the 4th Armored Division on the German forces surrounding Bastogne, four artillery battalions from the division used their guns to pound enemy positions. A supporting battalion of 155mm howitzers added weight to the American artillery barrage. Pictured are a battery of American self-propelled 155mm howitzers opening fire on enemy positions. *Patton Museum*

tillery of 75mm or over, and 332 vehicles of all types during the fighting.

In a general order addressed to the Third Army as well as the XIX Tactical Air Command on January 1, 1945, Patton congratulated them on a job well done: "From the bloody corridor at Avranches, to Brest, thence across

The 4th Armored Division's armored infantry, mounted in thin-skinned half-tracks, supported the attacking Shermans. While the tanks of the division managed to fight their way into Bastogne, the division's armored infantry lost most of its half-tracks to enemy fire. Many of the surviving infantrymen had to walk into Bastogne. Pictured are US Army half-tracks on the move. *Patton Museum*

France to the Saar, over the Saar into Germany, and now on to Bastogne, your record has been one of continous victory. Not only have you invariably defeated a cunning and ruthless enemy, but also you have overcome by your indomitable fortitude every aspect of terrain and weather. Neither heat nor dust nor floods nor snow have stayed your progress. The speed and brilliancy of your achievements are unsurpassed in military history.

"Recently I had the honor of receiving at the hands of the Twelfth Army Group Commander, Lieutenant General Omar N. Bradley, a second Oak Leaf Cluster to the DSM. This award was bestowed on me, not for what I have done, but because of what you have achieved. From the bottom of my heart I thank you.

"My New Year wish and sure conviction for you is that, under the protection of Almighty God and the inspired leadership of our President and the High Command, you will continue your victorious course to the end that tyranny and vice shall be eliminated, our dead comrades avenged, and peace restored to a war-weary world.

"In closing, I can find no fitter expression for my feelings than to apply to you the immortal words spoken by General Scott at Chapultepec when he said: 'Brave rifles, veterans, you have been baptized in fire and blood and have come out steel.'"

Of the nine roads and two rail lines running into the town, only the 4th Armored Division corridor was linked to the rest of Patton's Third Army. Combat Command B of the division fought northward, and Combat Command A to the east. By December 29, 1944, Bastogne was no longer besieged. The American tankers pictured all have their fingers crossed. No doubt, hoping the worst of the fighting was over. *Patton Museum*

The Germans still did not want to give up on taking Bastogne. On December 30, 1944, the east flank of the corridor cut into Bastogne by the 4th Armored Division was counter attacked by a German armored division supported by elements of two infantry divisions and remnants of a paratroop division. The Germans managed to reach the Belgian village of "Luterbois", just 1,200 yards from the main road leading to Bastogne. Pictured are two German Panther tanks on the move. *Patton Museum*

Artillery battalions of the 4th Armored Division poured the heaviest concentration they had ever fired into the small area the Germans were holding near Bastogne. In eight days, a total of 24,483 rounds from the division's 105mm howitzers were dumped into Luterbois and the surrounding woods. The Germans managed to hold onto Luterbois for one week, but it cost them dearly. They lost fifty-five tanks to the combination of fire from the 4th Armored and American ground-attack aircraft. Shown is a destroyed German Mark IV medium tank. *Patton Museum*

At the end of the Battle of the Bulge, the 4th Armored Division figured that in six months of fighting with the German Army, the division had taken 19,221 prisoners, killed and wounded just as many, destroyed 414 German tanks, 1,618 other vehicles, and 225 artillery pieces. In addition, twenty-six German planes had fallen to the division's anti-aircraft guns. Pictured is a US Army half-track mounting four .50-caliber machine guns in a power-operated turret. This weapon system was very effective in the antipersonnel role against German infantry formations. *Patton Museum*

The relief of Bastogne added another battle victory to the brilliant campaign record of the 4th Armored Division. In six months of fighting, the division had spearheaded virtually every Third Army offensive. Territory wrested from the German Army stretched from Normandy's hedgerows to the German border. Pictured is an M5A1 light tank passing through a burning town. *Patton Museum*

All attempts by the Germans to break through the 4th Armored Division to get back to Bastogne failed. Impaled on Bastogne, the German winter offensive died in the bleak, snow-covered fields of Belgium. Harassed on the ground and from the air, the Germans pulled back the mauled 5th and 6th panzer armies and the 7th Army. Pictured is a destroyed German self-propelled gun mounted on a Mark IV medium-tank chassis. *Patton Museum*

General Patton wrote to the commander of the 4th Armored Division, "The outstanding celerity of your movement and the unremitting, vicious, and skillful manner in which you pushed the attack, terminating at the end of four days and nights of incessant battle in the relief of Bastogne, constitutes one of the finest chapters in the glorious history of the US Army. You and the officers and men of your command are hereby commended for a superior performance." Pictured is a GI looking over a destroyed German StuG IV self-propelled gun. *Patton Museum*

On January 21, 1945, General Dwight Eisenhower wrote to the 4th Armored Division: "The 4th Armored Division is both feared and hated by German front-line troops because of its high combat efficiency. Some American POWs who could speak and understand German were told by enemy soldiers and officers that the 4th Armored Division has gained a reputation amongst the Wehrmacht of being a crack armored unit dangerous to oppose." Pictured is a graveyard of abandoned German 88mm guns. *Bill Hamberg*

CHAPTER SIX

PATTON'S MARCH ACROSS GERMANY

As February ended, all of the Third Army's tactical operations were inside of Germany. In March, the Third Army challenged the enemy on his home ground and inflicted a series of such disastrous defeats that he never recovered. The breathtaking sweep of the March operations compared with those of August 1944, when the Third Army's drive across France held the eyes of the world. The smashing of the Siegfried Line and the advance to the Rhine River, the charge across the enemy's rear that took the Third Army's spearheads far into Seventh Army's zone and led to the trapping of thousands of enemy troops in the Palatinate, the assault crossings of the Rhine for the first time in modern history, the penetration into central Germany—all these were highlights of the March operations.

Patton had always hoped that he would be the first to cross the Rhine River into Germany. Hungry for the glory that such an operation would bring to the Third Army and himself, he was very disappointed when Bradley's First Army managed to get across the Rhine River into Germany by capturing the Remagen bridge. Another reason that Patton wanted to cross the Rhine so quickly was to beat his old foe Field Marshal Montgomery to the prize. Patton was desperately worried that if Montgomery and his Eighth Army beat the American armies into Germany, Eisenhower would place Patton's Third Army as well as Bradley's First Army on the defense while funneling additional troops and supplies to the advance of the British Eighth Army.

Behind the Dragon's Teeth of the Siegfried line, the Germans had built a series of mutually supporting pillboxes similar to the one in this photo. Carefully positioned with excellent camouflage, these pillboxes could be deadly against attacking troops. The numerous streams along the Siegfried Line in combination with other difficult terrain features made this defensive line a tough nut to crack for the 4th Armored Division. *Patton Museum*

Patton's concerns about Montgomery beating the US Army into Germany were shared by other top American generals. General Omar Bradley had managed to get permission to increase the strength of First Army units in the Remagen bridgehead after a March 19 meeting with Eisenhower. He was also told to prepare his forces for a major breakout from the Remagen bridge area into Germany on March 23. This was to be the same date that Field Marshal

Montgomery's Rhine crossing was scheduled. Bradley quickly told Patton what was planned and added what Patton wanted to hear; cross the Rhine as soon as possible. Patton knew that the only way to beat Montgomery was to begin his advance on the night before.

Patton quickly ordered part of the 5th Infantry Division to cross the Rhine on the evening of the 23rd. In great haste, a force of over 7,000 engineer troops made elaborate preparations for supporting the infantry in their effort to get across the Rhine. The first assault waves were to transport bulldozers and air compressors so that work could begin immediately on cutting ramps for the amphibious trucks, nicknamed Ducks, and preparing bridge and ferry sites. Although the first waves were to paddle across in small assault boats, reinforcements were to cross in the Ducks. Once the first couple of waves were across the Rhine, Navy landing craft assisted by searchlights would help in the building of bridges.

German resistance to the crossing of the Rhine by Patton's troops was very weak. By midnight of the 22nd, Patton's infantry force was across the Rhine and ready to advance into the first group of German villages near the river itself. On the afternoon of the 23rd, the first of Patton's tanks and tank destroyers were being ferried across the river. On the evening of the 23rd, in a last attempt to push Patton's men behind the Rhine, a number of half-hearted counterattacks were launched by German infantry formations. They were beaten back in quick order by the soldiers of the Third Army.

Even while Patton's soldiers were beating back the German counterattacks. General Bradley announced to the world that Patton and his Third Army were inside of Germany. Two more crossings of the Rhine by the Third Army would be conducted in short order. The timing of Bradley's announcement was clearly aimed at taking the luster out of Field Marshall Montgomery's crossing of the Rhine which had started the morning of the 23rd.

Patton's 4th Armored Division would cross the Rhine on a treadway bridge beginning at 9:00 A.M. on the morning of March 24. It would take the division almost eighteen hours to get all 2,500 of their vehicles across.

Striking fast, the division sped more than twenty-five miles to the Main River. As the 4th

On January 29, 1945, three armored infantry battalions of the 4th Armored Division first glimpsed the dragon's teeth and pillboxes of the much vaunted German West Wall, or Siegfried Line; which were originally built as a series of earthen field fortifications facing the French Maginot Line. The Siegfried Line was never developed as fully as Hitler's Atlantic Wall. The best known feature of the Siegfried Line was its concrete tank obstacles known as "Dragon's Teeth." *Patton Museum*

Armored started to cross the Main River, a twenty-five car German train pulled into the local railroad station. The train cars were loaded with vehicles, artillery pieces, anti-aircraft guns, and small arms. Armored infantry hit the train with .30 and .50 caliber fire. When ammunition ran low, they stepped back and artillery barrages were called in. Shells rained up and down the train, shredding it as five cars were blown to pieces.

Next the division planned to used a 250-mile autobahn (freeway), which connected the German cities of Frankfurt and Chemnitz, as its general axis of movement deeper into Germany. Seventeen days after crossing the Main River, the 4th Armored Division was at the gates of Chemnitz. In a single day they had gone as many as forty miles, captured thirty-five German towns and 8,000 prisoners. Their route had taken them through the German industrial cities of Gotha, Weimar, Jena, and Gera. The Germans were surrendering in wholesale numbers without resistance.

In a twenty-four day drive from the German city of Worms to the city of Gotha, the 4th Armored Division killed 2,704 enemy soldiers, wounded 2,140, and took another 30,000 prisoners. The division managed to destroy 70 tanks, 39 locomotives and 1,134 railroad cars. The Germans were losing men

Rather than have the tanks of the 4th Armored Division impaled on the concrete dragon's teeth of the Siegfried Line, Patton assigned the half-tracked-equipped armored infantry battalions of the division to work through it. Once they were through, the 4th Armored Division was to follow their path and move on to Bitburg, Germany. *Patton Museum*

and supplies rapidly as the Allies pierced deeper into the country. On April 13, the 4th Armored Division advanced seventy-three miles against light resistance and overan German soldiers who quickly surrendered. The Division captured 2,601 prisoners that day and 4,097 the next.

On March 23, 1945, Patton had issued a message to his troops and the XIX Tactical Air Command, it read: "In the period from January 29 to March 22, 1945, you have wrested 6,484 square miles of territory from the enemy. You have taken 3,072 cities, towns, and villages, including among the former: Trier, Coblenz, Bingen, Worms, Mainz, Kaiserslautern, and Ludwigshafen.

"You have captured 140,112 enemy soldiers and have killed or wounded an additional 99,000, thereby eliminating practically all of the German 7th and 1st Armies. History records no greater achievement in so limited a time.

"This great campaign was only made possible by your disciplined valor, unswerving devotion to duty, doubled with the unparalleled audacity and speed of your advance on the ground; while from the air, the peerless fighter-bombers kept up a relentless round-the-clock attack upon the disorganized enemy.

"The world rings with your praises; better still, General Marshall, General Eisenhower, and General Bradley have all personally commended you. The highest honor I have attained is that of having my name coupled with yours in these great events.

"Please accept my heartfelt admiration and thanks for what you have done, and remember that your assault crossing over the Rhine at 2200 hours last night assures you of even greater glory to come.

On April 3, 1944, General Patton issued a letter of instruction to the men of the Third Army. Extracts from this letter give an excellent insight into Patton's thoughts on how an Army should be run:

II. DISCIPLINE

1. There is only one sort of discipline—perfect discipline. Men cannot have good battle discipline and poor administrative discipline.

2. Discipline is based on pride in the profession of arms, on meticulous attention to details, and on mutual respect and confidence. Discipline must be a habit so ingrained that it is stronger than the excitement of battle or the fear of death.

3. The history of our invariably victorious armies demonstrates that we are the best soldiers in the world. This should make your men proud. This should make you proud. This should imbue your units with unconquerable self-confidence and pride in demonstrated ability.

4. Discipline can only be obtained when all officers are so imbued with the sense of their awful obligation to their men and to their country that they cannot tolerate negligence. Officers who fail to correct errors or to praise excellence are valueless in peace and dangerous misfits in war.

5. Officers must assert themselves by example and by voice. They must be preeminent in courage, deportment, and dress.

6. One of the primary purposes of discipline is to produce alertness. A man who is so lethargic that he fails to salute will fall an easy victim to an enemy.

American GIs and officers were never very crazy about their M2 and M3 half-tracks. Beginning in 1942, American soldiers began referring to their thinly armored, open-topped half-tracks as "Purple Heart Boxes." Many divisional commanders felt that their infantry soldiers would be better off in trucks. Pictured is an American half-track that took a high-velocity round. One can only guess what happened to the vehicle's crew. *Patton Museum*

Colonel S. R. Hinds stated in a wartime report: "While our half-track vehicle is far superior to any other similar vehicle, it falls short of the required cross-country mobility. It should be the equal of a tank in this respect. I believe a full-track vehicle with slightly more armor on the sides is necessary in order to have the complete support of the armored infantry when most needed." This half-track is pictured in a winter camouflage paint scheme. *Patton Museum*

7. Combat experience has proven that ceremonies, such as formal guard mounts, formal retreat formations, and regular and supervised reveille formations are a great help and, in some cases, essential to prepare men and officers for battle, to give them that perfect discipline, that smartness of appearance, that alertness without which battles cannot be won.

III. TACTICAL USAGES

1. General

a. Combat Principles:

(1) There is no approved solution to any tactical situation.

(2) There is only one tactical principle which is not subject to change. It is: "To so use the means at hand to inflict the maximum amount of wounds, death, and destruction on the enemy in the minimum time."

(3) In battle, casualties vary directly with the time you are exposed to effective fire. Your own fire reduces the effectiveness and volume of the enemy's fire, while rapidity of attack shortens the time of exposure. A pint of sweat will save a gallon of blood.

(4) Battles are won by frightening the enemy. Fear is induced by inflicting death and wounds on him. Death and wounds are produced by fire. Fire from the rear is more deadly and three times more effective than fire from the front, but to get fire behind the enemy, you must hold him by frontal fire and move rapidly around his flank. Frontal attacks against prepared positions should be avoided if possible.

(5) "Catch the enemy by the nose with fire and kick him in the pants with fire emplaced through movement."

(6) Hit hard soon, that is with two battalions up in a regiment, or two divisions up in a corps, or two corps up in an army—the idea being to develop your maximum force at once before the enemy can develop his.

Lieutenant Colonel R. W. Jenna stated in a wartime report: "The US half-track is more versatile than the comparable German model, being used for a larger number of purposes: as personnel carrier, gun platform, AA gun mount, weapons carrier, and artillery ammunition carrier. The half-track serves to fill the needs of a number of vehicles employed by the Germans, who adopt different types of vehicles for different needs." Pictured on display in European military museum is this late-war German half-track. *Richard Pemberton*

7) You can never be too strong. Get every man and gun you can secure provided it does not unduly delay your attack. The German is the champion digger.

(8) The larger the force and the more violence you use in an attack, whether it be men, tanks, or ammunition, the smaller will be your proportional losses.

(9) Never yield ground. It is cheaper to hold what you have than to retake what you have lost. Never move troops to the rear for a rest or to reform at night, and in the daytime only where absolutely necessary. Such moves may produce a panic.

BELOW
Technician Grade Five Charles A. Horlick described a scary day on the Siegfried Line in his unit's history: "I was sent out one morning to stay with the radio in the command half-track. It wasn't long after I got into the track that the artillery started to come in. It started off with a heavy barrage that lasted about a half hour. Then it slowed down to a few shells every 15 minutes. As the time went on I got used to it, but I still sweated out the one that was going to join me in the half-track." Shown is one of the Patton Museum's half-tracks used in the annual living history show. *Michael Green*

Sergeant Glenn H. Murray recounted in his unit history: "We had gone through the first string of pillboxes and were firing on the second when an enemy artillery observer spotted our platoon and called for fire on our position. The tanks had no cover so I pulled up behind a pillbox and tried to find something to shoot at. The artillery was coming in, one would hit short and the next would go over us. I expected one to hit our tank any minute as there was about two feet of the turret showing above the pillbox. After about an hour of sweating it out, darkness set in and I was able to move to another position." Pictured is a Sherman tank covered with GIs crossing the Siegfried Line. *Patton Museum*

(10) Our mortars and our artillery are superb weapons when they are firing. When silent, they are junk—see that they fire!

IV. ARMOR

a. The primary mission of armored units is the attacking of infantry and artillery. The enemy's rear is the happy hunting ground for armor.

Use every means to get it there.

b. The tactical and technical training of our armored units is correct. Added emphasis should be put on tank crew training with a view to hitting the enemy first.

c. Against counter-attacks, the offensive use of armor striking the flank is decisive. Hence a deep penetration by infantry,

Sergeant Rex P. Taylor described an incident on the Siegfried Line in his unit's history: "Just at dark the infantry got an order to attack, so we had to go along as support. They moved into a patch of woods to the front of us and then called for us. When we reached them they had started back out as the Krauts were infiltrating their lines. However, we went on with the attack and fell into a tank trap. We had to stay there the rest off the night, setting at a 45deg angle. Having to traverse manually isn't an easy job, but we did it." Pictured stuck in a German tank trap is this M4 Sherman. *Patton Museum*

By February 22, 1945, parts of the Siegfried Line were broken by the piercing attacks of Patton's Third Army. In the first mass movement of 4th Armored Division troops into Germany, the division advanced forty miles in one day. On February 25, 1945, the division was less than two miles from Bitburg, Germany. By March 5, 1945, Bitburg was secured. Now the division's task was to reach for the Rhine River near the German city of Koblenz. Waiting for the order to move forward is a long column of Shermans. *Patton Museum*

whose rear is protected by armor, is feasible and safe.

d. There is no such thing as "Tank country" in a restrictive sense. Some types of country are better than others, but tanks have and can operate anywhere.

e. The integrity of armored divisions should be preserved through the use of GHQ [General Headquarters] tank battalions for special, close supporting missions with infantry. On such missions, the tanks should advance by bounds from cover to cover in rear of the infantry. They will only be exposed when the situation demands their intervention. In such cases, they will attack in close association with the infantry.

The end of Nazi Germany came in the first eight days of May. Patton's Third Army split Germany in half with an armor-spearheaded drive to the Czechoslovakian city of Pilsen. The eight days in May also brought collapse of the "national redoubt" myth. Even if the enemy had planned to make a last stand in the mountains of Bavaria and Austria, the Third Army's swift drive into the area ended this half-baked plan before it could be put into effect. During May, the

Third Army smashed relentlessly through all defenses the enemy threw in its path, playing its part in the destruction of the German war machine, which reached its climax with the unconditional surrender of all German armed forces on May 9, 1945. The final surrender was preceded by a mounting tide of piecemeal surrenders of battle groups, divisions, corps, and entire armies. Shortly before the war in Europe came to its end, Patton took the time to write another letter of instruction to the men of the Third Army. The letter itself was not issued until May 20, 1945, a few weeks after the Germans had surrendered. Extracts from this letter are still of great interest to see how Patton took such interest in the smaller items of military training and tactics:

TO: All Corps and Division Commanders

I. Use of armored divisions

1. The tactics prescribed for the use of armored divisions are correct, but owing to a lack of understanding of the word "Blitz," certain things are overemphasized, and other very much more important things do not receive sufficient emphasis.

2. To begin with, haste and speed are not synonymous. By this I mean that hasty attacks do not produce speedy successes or speedy advances because hasty attacks are not coordinated attacks. "Haste makes waste."

3. In an armored division, as in an infantry division, attacks must be coordinated; and the infantry, and the tanks, and the guns must work as a unit. Wherever possible, it is desirable that the guns operate under divisional control, and with their forward observers in tanks, immediately take under fire enemy anti-tank guns, and either reduce them or blind them with smoke or white phosphorus. Success depends upon the coordinated use of the guns and the tanks, with the guns paying particular attention to hostile artillery, and above all to anti-tank guns and observation posts.

4. The decision of whether the assault should be led by the infantry or the armored vehicles depends on circumstances. When operating against known antitank guns or against extensive antitank minefields, or where it is necessary to force a river crossing or a defile,

Only fifty-eight hours after taking Bitburg. The 4th Armored Division was at the banks of the Rhine, and was the eastern-most Allied unit on the western front. During those two and a half days, the division captured 6,000 prisoners, captured or destroyed more than 500 motor vehicles, killed 460 enemy soldiers, and wounded 240. Its own dead did not reach thirty. Pictured passing through a burning German town is an American M8 armored car. *Patton Museum*

the infantry must lead and the tanks follow as and when the situation is cleared.

5. When operating against small minefields or minefields composed of boot or other "S" type mines, or against normal infantry and artillery resistance, the tanks should lead. However, it is necessary to remember that the association between tanks and infantry in the case of armored divisions operating as such is not as intimate as that which I prescribed in "Tactical Use of Separate Tank Battalions." Still, cases will arise where tanks must act in close support with their armored infantry. Normally, the armored infantry and artillery is used either to make a hole or to open a door to permit the tank battalions to move forward. As soon as this occurs, the armored infantry and artillery must immediately follow them. All this is adequately covered in existing regulations.

6. When tanks are advancing, they must use their guns for what is known as reconnaissance by-fire; that is, they must shoot at any terrestrial objective behind which an antitank gun might be concealed and take these targets under fire at a range greater than that at which an antitank gun is effective—in other words, at a range greater than 2,000 yards. They should fire at these targets with high explosive or with white phosphorus, because if the enemy re- ceives such fire, he will consider himself discovered and reply at a range so great as to render him ineffective.

7. When tanks are passing or approaching hedges or walls, they should comb them with machine guns so as to remove the danger from close defense antitank grenades and sticky bombs.

8. When tanks use smoke or white phosphorus against infantry, tanks, or antitank guns, they should continue to fire into the smoke with high explosive or with machine guns if they are within range in order to prevent enemy movement.

9. Armored divisions should remember that many difficult open spaces can be passed with impunity if sufficient smoke is placed on the enemy guns and observation posts by the artillery of the division or through cooperation with the air force.

10. The quickest way to get to heaven is to advance across open ground swept by effective enemy antitank fire.

To summarize: We must take great and calculated risks in the use of armor, but we must not dive off the deep end without first determining whether the swimming pool is full of water.

You must never halt because some other unit is stuck. If you push on, you will release the pressure on the adjacent unit... Troops are never defeated by casualties but by lack of guts. Battles are won by a few brave men who refuse to fear and who push on. It should be our ambition to be members of this heroic group. More casualties occur among those who halt or go to the rear than among those who advance and advance firing.

Finally, all of us must have a desperate desire and determination to close with the enemy and destroy him.

11. In the Letter, as in those preceding it, I am not laying down inflexible rules. I am simply giving you my ideas. I must and do trust to your military experience, courage, and loyalty to make these ideas tangible. There are many ways of fighting, all of which are good if they are successful.

12. We are now entering the final stage of a great war, of a great victory! This victory can only be attained by the maximum use of all weapons, both physical and spiritual. It is the duty of all commanders to see that their men

Because of the gross inferiority of the US Army M5 and M5A1 light tanks armed with the puny 37mm antitank gun, a new light tank was fielded in Europe by December 1944. Designated the M24 Chaffee (named after General Adna Chaffee, "Father of the US Army's Armor Branch"), the vehicle was armed with a 75mm gun. The new tank was greeted with great delight by American tankers. Shown on display at Fort Hood, Texas, is this M24 Chaffee. *Bill Rosenmund*

are fully aware of the many vile deeds perpetrated upon civilization by Germans, and that they attack with the utmost determination, ferocity, and hate. I am sure that every man will do his duty, and I am therefore sure that victory is simply a question of when we find the enemy.

The 75mm gun on the M24 light tank fired the same ammunition as the Sherman's 75mm gun, but the gun itself weighted only 406lbs, half of what the older-generation gun on the Sherman did. The M24's gun was a modification of a lightweight US Army Air Forces 75mm gun that was designed to fit into the nose of a B-25H Mitchell bomber. Powered by two Cadillac V-8 gasoline engines, the vehicle's top speed was 35mph. Pictured going up a very steep slope is an M24 Chaffee. *Patton Museum*

LEFT TOP
Despite the big improvement the M24 light tank was to the earlier M5 and M5A1 light tanks, it still did not compare well with late-war German tanks such as the Panther. According to Tank driver Henry V. Strobe who stated in a wartime report: "On March 12, 1945, I drove my light tank [M24] in a recognition demonstration. A captured German Mark V Panther was participating in the training. I found that the Panther could turn faster, go as fast on ordinary terrain, and presented a lower silhouette than my M24 light tank. Still on display in a small Belgian town is this German Panther tank.
Andreas Kirchhoff

LEFT BOTTOM
First Lieutenant Harold A. Shields describes a combat engagement in a wartime report: "Upon taking the battalion objective at Fichlen, Germany, three of our medium tanks were knocked out by a German self-propelled gun (a long-barreled 75 on a Mark IV chassis). I took this self-propelled gun under fire with my platoon of M24 light tanks at 800 yards. The platoon fired a total of twenty-five rounds, the majority of which were AP [armor piercing]. None of the AP pierced the front slope plate of the self-propelled." Pictured on display at the German Army Tank Museum is this German late-war self-propelled gun armed with a high-velocity antitank gun. *Andreas Kirchhoff*

Captain John B. Roller Jr. described another combat engagement: "In our only clash with armor, one of my M24s engaged a German Mark IV frontally at 200 yards. The M24 got off the first rounds, hitting the Mark IV on the front and ricocheting off. This apparently stunned the crew, since we were able to fire a second round that set the Mark IV on fire." On display at the Patton Museum is this M24 Chaffee. *Michael Green*

Twenty M26 Pershing tanks reached Europe in January 1945. The tank was named in honor of Patton's friend and mentor in his early years, General John "Black Jack" Pershing, commander of all US Army troops in Europe during World War I. The Pershing weighed about forty-six tons and was powered by the same Ford V-8 gasoline engine found in the M4A3 Sherman. Armor thickness was over four inches on the front of the vehicle's turret. Pictured in a postwar training exercise is this view of a Pershing with infantry on its rear deck. *Patton Museum*

The only tank that was put into the field by the American armored force during World War II that stood the slightest chance in a head-to-head battle with late-war German tanks was the M26 Pershing heavy tank. Unfortunately, the development of the M26 was a long and complicated program. The result was that only a handful of Pershing tanks made it to Europe before the war ended. With fairly thick frontal armor and a 90mm gun, the M26 was far superior to the Sherman tank series. Pictured on display in Europe is this M26 Pershing tank. *Michael Green*

American tankers had long awaited the M26 Pershing with mixed feelings, as Second Lieutenant Robert V. McQuillen stated in a wartime report: "Have not seen the M26 tank; however, the 90mm gun is believed to be the best antitank weapon we have. This belief is formed through observation of the 90mm tank destroyers." Pictured is a Pershing on display in the Patton Museum. *Michael Green*

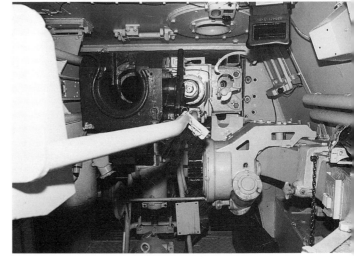

Sergeant Moore and his tank crew stated in a wartime report: "My opinion of the 90mm gun is that it is a good gun. If it just had a little more muzzle velocity, it could knock out anything that the Germans have. I have never seen the M26 with the 90mm gun on it, but if it is as good as the ones on the T.D. it is the answer to a tankman's prayer. Against the Mark V our T.D. with a 90mm gun is pretty good but our guns just don't stand up to the Jerry guns." This view looking into the turret of a Panther tank shows the breech end of the vehicle's deadly 75mm gun. *Andreas Kirchhoff*

Leading Patton's Third Army deep into Germany, the 4th Armored Division was in Bavaria by late April 1945. On May 3, 1945, news came that Berlin had been captured by the Red Army. Because German forces were still fighting in Czechoslovakia, the division headed that way on May 6, 1945. On May 7, 1945, the German High Command had unconditionally surrendered to the Allies. A lot of brave American tankers and their vehicles had been left across Europe's landscape by the end of the war in Europe. *Patton Museum*

CHAPTER SEVEN

PATTON'S POSTWAR THOUGHTS

With the war in Europe ending in May 1945, Patton now had more time to think about his wartime experiences and the impressions he had formed. Sometime between the end of May 1945 and December 9, 1945 (when Patton was critically injured in a car crash near Mannheim, Germany) he took the time to write down his thoughts for future American military leaders. Patton titled his paper as "Helpful Hints for Hopeful Heroes." Some of the more interesting extracts from that document are reproduced here:

REFLECTIONS AND SUGGESTIONS OR, IN A LIGHTER VEIN, HELPRUL HINTS TO HOPEFUL HEROES

Probably there is nothing original in what I shall now put down because war is an ancient subject and I, an ancient man, have studied and practiced it for over forty years. So, what appears to me as original thought may be simply subconscious memories.

In this classic picture of Patton we see him with all four of his stars. Patton was a little upset that he didn't receive his fourth star until near the end of the war in Europe. Patton did state that "Ike was quite apologetic about the four-star business, but has, however, good reasons. That is, you must maintain the hierarchy of Command or else relieve them, and he had no reason for relieving them. At the moment I am having so much fun fighting that I don't care what my rank is." *Patton Museum*

**PART I
CONCERNING THE SOLDIER**

The soldier is the Army. No army is better than its soldiers. The soldier is also a citizen. In fact, the highest obligation and privilege of citizenship is that of bearing arms for one's country. Hence it is a proud privilege to be a soldier... a good soldier. Anyone in any walk of life who is content with mediocrity is untrue to himself and to American tradition. To be a good soldier a man must have discipline, self respect, pride in his unit and in his country, a high sense of duty and obligation to his comrades and to his superiors, and self confidence born of demonstrated ability.

This portrait of Patton, done at the end of the war, shows him with all four stars and his well-known ivory-handled pistols. These pistols became one of Patton's trademarks. They are now on display at the Patton Museum of Cavalry and Armor located at Fort Knox, Kentucky. *Patton Museum*

Patton did not like the Russians at all, but is pictured here with a top-ranking Soviet Army general at a postwar parade. Patton once stated, that "I believe that by taking a strong attitude with the Russians, they will back down. We have already yielded too much to their Mongolian nature." *Patton Museum*

RIGHT
Patton in a letter describes a famous incident: "I drove to the Rhine River and went across on the pontoon bridge. I stopped in the middle to take a piss and then picked up some dirt on the far side in emulation of William the Conqueror." *Patton Museum*

There has been and is now a great deal of talk about discipline, but few people, in or out of the Army, know what it is or why it is necessary.

When a man enters the Army he leaves home, usually for the first time, and also he leaves behind him the inhibitions resulting from his respect for the opinion of his parents and his friends which inhibitions, unknown to himself, have largely guided his existence. When he joins a unit and lacks this corrective influence he is apt to slip in morals, in neatness, and in energy. Administrative discipline must replace the absent inhibitions.

All human beings have an innate resistance to obedience. Discipline removes this resistance and, by constant repetition, makes obedience habitual and subconscious. Where would an undisciplined football team get? The players react subconsciously to the signals. They must, because the split second required for thought would give the enemy the jump.

Battle is much more exciting that football. No sane man is not afraid in battle, but discipline produces in him a form of vicarious courage which, with his manhood, makes for victory. Self respect grows directly from discipline. The Army saying "Who ever saw a dirty soldier with a medal?" is largely true. Pride, in turn, stems from self respect and from the knowledge that the soldier is an American. The sense of duty and obligation to his comrades and superiors comes from a knowledge

of reciprocal obligation and from the sharing of the same way of life. Self confidence, the greatest military virtue, results from the demonstrated ability derived from the acquisition of all the preceding qualities and from exercise in the use of weapons.

It is an unfortunate and, to me, tragic fact that in our attempts to prevent war we have taught our people to belittle the heroic qualities of the soldier. They do not realize that, as Shakespeare put it, the pursuit of "The bubble reputation even at the carrion's mouth" is not only a good military characteristic but also very helpful to the young man when bullets and shells are whistling and cracking around him. Much more could be done if the women of America would praise their heroes and if pa-

A photo of Patton taken shortly after the end of the war in Europe. Patton is giving a farewell speech to the soldiers of his Third Army. The large A on the front of the wooden platform is part of the widely known insignia of the Third Army. The white

A on a blue background, circled by a red "O" stood for Army of Occupation. Right after World War I ended in 1918, the American Third Army held the US zone on the Rhine in Germany. *Patton Museum*

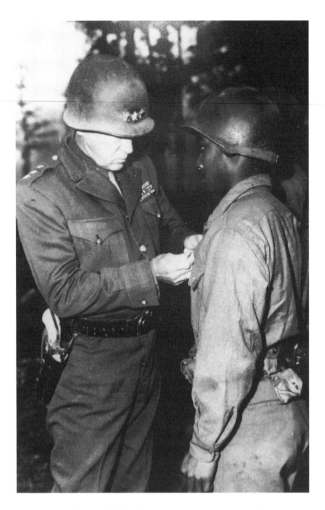

In November 1944, Patton gave a speech to the men of the 761st Tank Battalion. This was one of only three all-Negro tank battalions to be formed during World War II. Patton stated: "You're the first Negro tankers to ever fight in the US Army. I would never have asked for you if you weren't good. I have nothing but the best in my Army. I don't care what color you are, so long as you go up there and kill those Kraut sonsabitches. Everybody has their eyes on you and is expecting great things from you. Most of all, your race is looking forward to you. Don't let them down, and, damn you, don't let me down." *Patton Museum*

pers would publish the citations of soldiers in their home towns and further, if foolish ideas of security did not make the citations so unrealistic. Perhaps not returning soldiers of this way may correct this very unfortunate situation.

Surrender: Any soldier who surrenders with arms in his hands is not doing his duty to his country and is selling himself short because the living conditions of the Prisoner of War are extremely bad. Also the Prisoner of War is apt to become the unintended victim of our own air and artillery bombardments. If the enemy indicates a desire to surrender, make him come to you with his hands up. Don't advance towards him and do not stop shooting until he does so surrender himself. When the enemy has surrendered he must be treated in accordance with the rules of land warfare.

Miscellaneous Notes

During mobile operations it is better to use secondary roads for the axis of advance than primary roads. In the first place, the secondary roads are less apt to be thoroughly guarded, and, in the second place, there will be fewer demolitions on them. The primary roads must be repaired as promptly as possible behind the fighting front to secure efficient supply lines.

Obstacles and demolitions unless defended are of little value. It is not necessary to sit on a demolition or obstacle in order to defend it because the enemy will place fire there. These points are best defended from a distance of several hundred yards for small arms and from normal artillery range for that arm.

Patton stated in a postwar report: "In cold weather General Officers must be careful not to appear to dress more warmly than the men." *Patton Museum*

Administrative discipline is the index of combat discipline. Any commander who is unwilling or unable to enforce administrative discipline will be incapable of enforcing combat discipline. An experienced officer can tell by a very cursory administrative inspection of any unit the calibre of its commanding officer.

The more senior the officer the more time he has. Therefore, the senior should go forward to visit the junior rather than call the junior back to see him. The exception to this is when it is necessary to collect several commanders for the formulation of a coordinated plan. In that case, the juniors should report to the superior headquarters.

PART IV
COMMAND

Don't delay; The best is the enemy of the good. By this I mean that a good plan violently executed now is better than a perfect plan next week. War is a very simple thing and the determining characteristics are self confidence, speed, and audacity. None of these things can ever be perfect but they can be good.

Reports: In war, nothing is ever as bad or as good as it is reported to higher headquarters. Any reports which emanate from a unit after dark, that is, where the knowledge has been obtained after dark, should be viewed with skepticism by the next higher unit. Reports by wounded men are always exaggerated and favor the enemy.

Identification: Legible unit signs in the clear are more valuable than dangerous, and they should be placed where they can be seen.

Sand table exercises by staffs up to and including Corps or Army, even on the most rudimentary type of sand table, are extremely helpful prior to an attack.

Patton stated in a postwar report: "When a unit has been alerted for inspection do not fail to inspect it and inspect it thoroughly. Further, do not keep it waiting. When soldiers have gone to the trouble of getting ready to be inspected they deserve the compliment of a visit." *Patton Museum*

General Officers: There are more tired Division Commanders than there are tired Divisions.

Tired Officers are always pessimists. Remember this when evaluating reports.

Generals must never show doubt, discouragement, or fatigue.

Generals should adhere to one type of dress so that soldiers will recognize them. They must always be very neat.

In cold weather General Officers must be careful not to appear to dress more warmly than the men.

Commanders and their staffs should visit units two echelons below their own and their maps should be so kept. In other words, Corps Commanders or their staffs should visit Division and Regimental Command Posts; the Division Commander should visit Regimental and Battalion Command Posts; the visits above referred to are for commmand purposes. What might be called inspirational visits should go further up. The more senior the officer who appears with a very small unit at the front, the better the effect on the troops. If some danger is involved in the visit its value is enhanced.

When speaking to a junior about the enemy confronting him, always understate their strength. You do this because the person in contact with the enemy invariably overestimates their strength to himself so if you understate it you probably hit the approximate fact, and also enhance your junior's self confidence.

All officers and particularly General Officers must be vitally interested in everything that interests the soldier. Usually you will gain a great deal of knowledge by being interested, but even if you do not, the fact that you appear interested has a very high morale influence on the soldier.

In my experience all very successful commanders are prima donnas and must be so treated. Some officers require urging, others require suggestion, very few have to be restrained.

A General Officer who will invariably assume the responsibility for failure, whether he deserves it or not, and invariably give the credit for success to others, whether they deserve it or not, will achieve outstanding success. In any case, letters of commendation and General Orders presenting to the command the glory and magnitude of their achievements have great influence on morale.

Corps and Army Commanders must make it a point to be physically seen by as many individuals of their command as possible—certainly by all combat soldiers. The best way to do this is to assemble the divisions, either as a whole or in separate pieces, and make a short talk.

When a unit leaves your command, if its performance at all justifies it, a letter of farewell and commendation to the unit should be sent.

During battle it is very important to visit frequently hospitals containing newly wounded men. Before starting such an inspection the officer in charge of the hospital should inform the inspecting general which wards contain men whose conduct does not merit compliments.

Generals and their principal staff officers should keep diaries.

Avoid the vicious habit of naming the next superior as the author of any adverse criticism while claiming all complimentary remarks for yourself.

LEFT TOP
According to Patton: "Corps and Army Commanders must make it a point to be physically seen by as many individuals of their command as possible, certainly by all combat soldiers." Pictured is Patton visiting his troops in the field. *Patton Museum*

LEFT BOTTOM
One of the best known American-built vehicles to come out of World War II was the jeep. Almost 400,000 were built during the war years. Originally designed as a reconnaissance car that could replace Army motorcycles, the jeep proved to be so useful that it soon found itself performing a wide range of duties with every branch of the American military. One of the most noticeable roles for the wartime jeep was as a command car for general officers. Shown is a side view of one of Patton's specially modified wartime jeeps. *Patton Museum*

NEXT PAGE TOP
According to a postwar report written shortly before his death, Patton stated: "Trucks arranged for sleeping accommodations for General and Senior Staff Officers save much time and promote efficiency. In addition, in the forward Echelon there should be three large office trailers, one for the Commanding General and Chief of Staff." Pictured during World War II is Patton stepping out of his personal mobile home (a converted 6x6 Army truck). *Patton Museum*

NEXT PAGE BOTTOM
During World War II, Patton's Third Army sent back to the US Army Armored School at Fort Knox, Kentucky, a great deal of captured enemy equipment for technical evaluation. In the postwar period these wartime vehicles and equipment formed the beginnings of the now famous Patton Museum of Cavalry and Armor located at Fort Knox. These two pictures taken during the 1950s show the museum collection in a now-torn-down older building. The museum is presently located in a state-of-the-art building located right off the main highway to the entrance of Fort Knox. *Patton Museum*

This postwar picture taken at the Patton Museum shows one of Patton's wartime jeeps on display. Notice the ever-present air horns on the hood. *Patton Museum*

On December 9, 1945, Patton was in Germany on his way to go bird shooting with his chief of staff, Major General Gay. Patton's driver was caught by surprise when a large US Army truck tried to make a left turn right in front of them. Patton's 1939 Cadillac sedan slammed into the side of the truck. While General Gay and Patton's driver's were unhurt in the accident. Patton had broken his neck and was taken away to the hospital in Heidelberg, Germany. Pictured right after the accident is the front end of Patton's Cadillac. The repaired Cadillac that Patton was riding in on that day is on display at the Patton Museum of Cavalry and Armor. *Patton Museum*

LEFT TOP
Patton died in his sleep of a blood clot twelve days after his car accident on December 21, 1945. In charge of Patton's funeral arrangements was Lieutenant General Geoffrey Keyes. Patton would lay in state at a large mansion in Heidelberg, Germany. Pictured is Patton laying in state flanked by military policemen on either side of his casket. *Patton Museum*

LEFT BOTTOM
The pallbearers at Patton's funeral included Master Sergeant William G. Meeks. Meeks on the left front of the casket had been Patton's orderly for over eight years and was close friends with both Patton and his wife. *Patton Museum*

To carry Patton's casket during the funeral and burial ceremony, two half-tracks were modified by a US Army Ordnance Company located between Heidelberg and Mannheim, Germany.

Of the two vehicles, one was to be used as the primary carrier and the other would serve as a standby in the event of mechanical failure. *Patton Museum*

★ ★ ★ ★
Bibliography

This work is essentially a picture book. Both the text and captions are drawn mainly from a wide variety of official United States Army publications too numerous to list. Most of them date from the World War II era or shortly thereafter. Much of the official material consists of reports put together by unnamed authors. Other sources consist of division histories published shortly after the war in Europe ended and were themselves based on unit after-action reports. A large amount of background material was also acquired from back issues of "Armor Magazine" (The Magazine of Mobile Warfare). Another heavily used source for this book was the official history of the US Army in World War II. Published by the US Army Center for Military History in a multi-volume set during the early 1960s.

★ ★ ★ ★
Index

I Armored Corps, 5, 8, 12, 53
II Corps, 30, 32, 33
V Corps, 108
VIII Corps, 67, 68, 109
XII Air Support Command, 59
XII Corps, 67, 85, 86, 88, 108, 111, 112
XV Corps, 67
XIX Tactical Air Command, 115, 126
XX Corps, 67, 85, 86, 88, 109

1st Armored Division, 6, 8, 31, 33
1st Division (Canada), 53
1st Infantry Division, 57, 62
2nd Armored Division, 6, 8, 9, 20, 55, 57, 58, 59
3rd Infantry Division, 59
4th Armored Division, 5, 69, 74, 80, 81, 82, 83, 109,
    111, 112, 113, 114, 125, 126
5th Infantry Division, 86, 109, 125
6th Armored Division, 5, 69, 70, 73, 74, 75, 76, 110
10th Armored Division, 109
11th Panzer Division, 86
26th Infantry Division, 109, 111
35th Infantry Division, 110
66th Armored Regiment, 8
67th Armored Regiment, 57
80th Infantry Division, 86, 109, 111
90th Infantry Division, 86
95th Infantry Division, 86
344th Tank Battalion, 8

Combat Command A, 10, 58, 59, 113

Combat Command B, 10, 58, 59, 113
Eighth Army (British), 60, 61, 62, 124
Fifth Panzer Army, 108
First Army (US), 64, 65, 72, 80
Seventh Army (US), 53, 59, 61, 62, 64, 86, 124
Sixth SS Panzer Army, 108
Task Force A, 69, 70
Third Army (US), 5, 7, 67, 68, 71, 72, 73, 74, 78, 80,
    82, 84, 85, 86, 88, 89, 109, 112, 113, 114, 115, 124,
    125, 127, 132, 133
Twelfth Army Group, 116
Hermann Goering Panzer Division, 57

Bradley, Gen. Omar, 33, 64, 65, 70, 71, 80, 116, 124,
    125, 126
Chaffee, Maj. Gen. Adna R., 6, 7, 8
Crittenberger, Brig. Gen. Willis D., 12
Cunningham, Adm. Andrew Browne, 53
Earnest, Brig. Gen. Herbert L., 69
Eisenhower, Gen. Dwight, 19, 33, 53, 60, 63, 65, 66,
    68, 71, 124, 126
Fredendall, Maj. Gen. Lloyd R., 30
Gaffey, Maj. Gen. Hugh T., 112
Gardiner, Col. Henry, 30
Gillem, Gen. Alvin C. Jr., 60
Grow, Gen. Robert, 70, 73
Middleton, Gen. Troy, 73
Montgomery, Gen. Bernard, 53, 61, 65, 124, 125
Tedder, Air Marshal Arthur W., 53
Ward, Maj. Gen. Orlando, 30
Wood, Gen. John S., 73, 111, 112